An Explanation of the Small Catechism

BY JOSEPH STUMP, D.D.

PREFACE

This book aims to present both an analysis of Luther's Small Catechism and a clear, concise, yet reasonably full explanation of its contents. It is an attempt, upon the basis of twenty years' experience and a study of the literature of the subject, to meet the peculiar wants of the catechetical class in our Lutheran Church in America. The object of the book is twofold: first, to furnish an outline of teaching which the pastor may use as a guide in his oral explanation and questioning; and secondly, to furnish a sufficiently complete summary by means of which the catechumens may review the lesson and fix its salient points in their minds. No text-book can, of course, adequately supply the parenetical side of the catechetical instruction or take the place of the living exposition by the pastor. But it can and should support his work, so that what he explains at one meeting may not be forgotten before the next meeting, but may be fixed in the minds of the catechumens by study at home.

Since the task of the pastor in catechization is not only to impart religious instruction, but to impart it on the basis of that priceless heritage of our Church, Luther's Small Catechism, the explanation here offered follows the catechism closely. The words of the catechism are printed in heavy-faced type and are used as headings wherever possible; and thus the words of the catechism may be traced as a thread running through the entire explanation.

Wherever he deemed it necessary, the author has added a fuller explanation of the text of the catechism than that which Luther gives, and has supplemented its contents with such additional matter as the needs of our catechumens require. He does not agree with those catechetical writers who maintain that the pastor, in his catechization, must confine himself to an explanation of *Luther's explanation*. Such a principle would exclude from the catechetical class much which our catechumens should be taught. But all such additional matters are introduced under an appropriate head as an organic part of the whole explanation, thus preserving its unity.

This book is written in the thetical form instead of the traditional form of questions and answers. There is nothing in the nature of catechization which would require the use of the interrogative form in such a text-book, and accordingly the thetical form has for years been employed by numerous writers of text-books for the catechetical class in Germany. While questions have an important place in catechetical instruction, the matter and not the form is the vital thing. Catechization is *not a method* of instruction by means of questions and answers. Neither the original meaning of the word nor the history of catechization justifies such a definition. (See my article, "A Brief History of Catechization," in the Lutheran Church Review, January, 1902; comp. v. Zezschwitz: System der christl.-kirchl. Katechetik, vol. i. pp. 17 seq., and vol. ii., 2. 1., pp. 3 seq.) And since Christian truth is not something to be brought forth from the mind of the child by means of questions, but something divinely revealed and hence *to be communicated* to the child, the most natural form in which to set it before him in a text-book is the thetical. Luther's catechism itself is, indeed, in the form of questions and answers. But his catechism is confessional as well as didactic, and its words, memorized by the catechumen, are to become a personal confession of faith. The explanations of a text-book, on the other hand, are not to be memorized, but are meant to aid the catechumen in grasping the *thoughts* of the catechism. For this purpose, the thetical form is better than the interrogative, because the explanation is not continually broken by questions, and is thus better adapted to give the catechumens a connected idea of the doctrines taught.

Each chapter of this explanation is followed by a number of questions. After the pastor has explained a lesson at one meeting, the catechumens should prepare themselves to give an answer to the printed questions *in their own words* at the next meeting. The pastor may, of course, substitute other questions, assign additional ones, or eliminate some. The proof passages for the teachings set forth are cited in the margin. The more important passages, particularly those which the catechumens may be expected to memorize, are specially indicated by a dagger (+), and are printed in full at the end of the chapter. The use of a Scripture lesson is, of course, optional with the pastor. One is indicated, however, for each chapter, and may be read in class or be assigned to the catechumens to be read at home. The Scriptural illustrations are cited for the convenience of the pastor in his oral exposition. The division into chapters has been regulated by the subject-matter, and will, it is hoped, aid in the survey of the contents of the book as a whole. It is not intended that each chapter shall necessarily constitute one lesson. Some lessons will doubtless include only a part of a chapter, while others will include several chapters, as the pastor may determine.

While the author, in the preparation of this explanation of Luther's catechism, has gone his own way, careful consideration has been given to the voice of those whose study of the problems involved entitled them to be heard. Luther's other catechetical writings, the standard theoretical works on Catechetics, and numerous monographs have been constantly at hand. Explanations of the catechism for the use of pastors and teachers have been freely consulted,—among others, those of Schuetze, Fricke, Mehliss, Kahle, Zuck, Kaftan, v. Zezschwitz, Palmer, Harnack, Nissen, Hempel, Schultze, Th. Hardeland, O. Hardeland, Nebe, Buchrucker, and Cremer. Acknowledgment is due also to the authors of numerous American and German text-books and helps for the catechetical class, whose works have been carefully scanned, in order that the fruits of past experience and the best results of former labors in this field might, if possible, be embodied in this work.

May the Lord bless this explanation of Luther's Small Catechism to the upbuilding of His kingdom and the glory of His name.

JOSEPH STUMP.
PHILLIPBURG, N. J.,
REFORMATION DAY, 1907.

LUTHER'S PREFACE

Martin Luther to all faithful and godly Pastors and Preachers: Grace, Mercy and Peace, in Jesus Christ, our Lord!

The deplorable condition in which I found religious affairs during a recent visitation of the congregations, has impelled me to publish this Catechism, or statement of the Christian doctrine, after having prepared it in very brief and simple terms. Alas! what misery I beheld! The people, especially those who live in the villages, seem to have no knowledge whatever of Christian doctrine, and many of the pastors are ignorant and incompetent teachers. And, nevertheless, they all maintain that they are Christians, that they have been baptized, and that they have received the Lord's Supper. Yet they cannot recite the Lord's Prayer, the Creed, or the Ten Commandments; they live as if they were irrational creatures, and now that the Gospel has come to them, they grossly abuse their Christian liberty.

Ye bishops! what answer will ye give to Christ for having so shamefully neglected the people, and paid no attention to the duties of your office? I invoke no evil on your heads. But you withhold the cup in the Lord's Supper, insist on the observance of your human laws, and yet, at the same time, do not take the least interest in teaching the people the Lord's Prayer, the Creed, the Ten Commandments, or any other part of the word of God. Woe unto you!

Wherefore I beseech you in the Name of God, my beloved brethren, who are pastors or preachers, to engage heartily in the discharge of the duties of your office, to have mercy on the people who are entrusted to your care, and to assist us in introducing the Catechism among them, and especially among the young. And if any of you do not possess the necessary qualifications, I beseech you to take at least the following forms, and read them, word for word, to the people, on this wise:—

In the first place; let the preacher take the utmost care to avoid all changes or variations in the text and wording of the Ten Commandments, the Lord's Prayer, the Creed, the Sacraments, etc. Let him, on the contrary, take each of the forms respectively, adhere to it, and repeat it anew, year after year. For young and inexperienced people cannot be successfully instructed, unless we adhere to the same text or the same forms of expression. They easily become confused, when the teacher at one time employs a certain form of words and expressions, and, at another, apparently with a view to make improvements, adopts a different form. The result of such a course will be, that all the time and labor which we have expended will be lost.

This point was well understood by our venerable fathers, who were accustomed to use the same words in teaching the Lord's Prayer, the Creed, and the Ten Commandments. We, too, should follow this plan when we teach these things, particularly in the case of the young and ignorant, not changing a single syllable, nor introducing any variations when, year after year, we recur to these forms and recite them anew before our hearers.

Choose, therefore, the form of words which best pleases you, and adhere to it perpetually. When you preach in the presence of intelligent and learned men, you are at liberty to exhibit your knowledge and skill, and may present and discuss these subjects in all the varied modes which are at your command. But when you are teaching the young, retain the same form and manner without change; teach them, first of all, the Ten Commandments, the Creed, the Lord's Prayer, etc., always presenting the same words of the text, so that those who learn can repeat them after you, and retain them in the memory.

But if any refuse to receive your instructions, tell them plainly that they deny Christ and are not Christians; such persons shall not be admitted to the Lord's Table, nor present a child for baptism, nor enjoy any of our Christian privileges, but are to be sent back to the pope and his agents, and, indeed, to Satan himself. Their parents and employers should, besides, refuse to furnish them with food and drink, and notify them that the government was disposed to banish from the country all persons of such a rude and intractable character.

For although we cannot, and should not, compel them to exercise faith, we ought, nevertheless, to instruct the great mass with all diligence, so that they may know how to distinguish between right and wrong in their conduct towards those with whom they live, or among whom they desire to earn their living. For whoever desires to reside in a city, and enjoy the rights and privileges which its laws confer, is also bound to know and obey those laws. God grant that such persons may become sincere believers! But if they remain dishonest and vicious, let them at least withhold from public view the vices of their hearts.

In the second place; when those whom you are instructing have become familiar with the words of the text, it is time to teach them to understand the meaning of those words, so that they may become acquainted with the object and purport of the lesson. Then proceed to another of the following forms, or, at your pleasure, choose any other which is brief, and adhere strictly to the same words and forms of expression in the text, without altering a single syllable; besides, allow yourself ample time for the lessons. For it is not necessary that you should, on the same occasion, proceed from the beginning to the end of the several parts; it will be more profitable if you present them separately, in regular succession. When the people have, for instance, at length correctly understood the First Commandment, you may proceed to the Second, and so continue. By neglecting to observe this mode, the people will be overburdened, and be prevented from understanding and retaining in memory any considerable part of the matter communicated to them.

In the third place; when you have thus reached the end of this Short Catechism, begin anew with the Large Catechism, and by means of it furnish the people with fuller and more comprehensive explanations. Explain here at large every Commandment, every

Petition, and, indeed, every part, showing the duties which they severally impose, and both the advantages which follow the performance of those duties, and also the dangers and losses which result from the neglect of them. Insist in an especial manner on such. Commandments or other parts as seem to be most of all misunderstood or neglected by your people. It will, for example, be necessary that you should enforce with the utmost earnestness the Seventh Commandment, which treats of stealing, when you are teaching workmen, dealers and even farmers and servants, inasmuch as many of these are guilty of various dishonest and thievish practices. So, too, it will be your duty to explain and apply the Fourth Commandment with great diligence, when you are teaching children and uneducated adults, and to urge them to observe order, to be faithful, obedient and peaceable, as well as to adduce numerous instances mentioned in the Scriptures, which show that God punished such as were guilty in these things, and blessed the obedient.

Here, too, let it be your great aim to urge magistrates and parents to rule wisely, and to educate the children, admonishing them, at the same time, that such duties are imposed on them, and showing them how grievously they sin if they neglect them. For in such a case they overthrow and lay waste alike the kingdom of God and the kingdom of the world, acting as if they were the worst enemies both of God and man. And show them very plainly the shocking evils of which they are the authors, when they refuse their aid in training up children to be pastors, preachers, writers, etc., and set forth that on account of such sins God will inflict an awful punishment upon them. It is, indeed, necessary to preach on these things; for parents and magistrates are guilty of sins in this respect, which are so great that there are no terms in which they can be described. And truly, Satan has a cruel design in fostering these evils.

Finally; inasmuch as the people are now relieved from the tyranny of the pope, they refuse to come to the Lord's Table, and treat it with contempt. On this point, also, it is very necessary that you should give them instructions, while, at the same time, you are to be guided by the following principles: That we are to compel no one to believe, or to receive the Lord's Supper; that we are not to establish any laws on this point, or appoint the time and place; but that we should so preach as to influence the people, without any law adopted, by us, to urge, and, as it were, to compel us who are pastors, to administer the Lord's Supper to them. Now this object may be attained, if we address them in the following manner; It is to be feared that he who does not desire to receive the Lord's Supper at least three or four times during the year, despises the Sacrament, and is no Christian. So, too, he is no Christian, who neither believes nor obeys the Gospel; for Christ did not say: "Omit or despise this," but "This do ye, as oft as ye drink it," etc. He commands that this should be done, and by no means be neglected and despised. He says: "This do."

Now he who does not highly value the Sacrament, shows thereby that he has no sin, no flesh, no devil, no world, no death, no danger, no hell; that is to say, he does not believe that such evils exist, although he may be deeply immersed in them, and completely belong to the devil. On the other hand, he needs no grace, no life, no Paradise, no heaven, no Christ, no God, no good thing. For if he believed that he was involved in such evils, and that he was in need of such blessings, he could not refrain from receiving the Sacrament, wherein aid is afforded against such evils, and, again, such blessings are bestowed. It will not be necessary to compel him by the force of any law to approach the Lord's Table; he will hasten to it of his own accord, will compel himself to come, and indeed urge you to administer the Sacrament to him.

Hence, you are by no means to adopt any compulsory law in this case, as the Pope has done. Let it simply be your aim to set forth distinctly the advantages and losses, the wants and the benefits, the dangers and the blessings, which are to be considered in connection with the Sacrament; the people will, doubtless, then seek it without urgent demands on your part. If they still refuse to come forward, let them choose their own ways, and tell them that those who do not regard their own spiritual misery, and do not desire the gracious help of God, belong to Satan. But if you do not give such solemn admonitions, or if you adopt odious compulsory laws on the subject, it is your own fault if the people treat the Sacrament with contempt. Will they not necessarily be slothful, if you are silent and sleep? Therefore consider the subject seriously, ye Pastors and Preachers! Our office has now assumed a very different character from that which it bore under the Pope; it is now of a very grave nature, and is very salutary in its influence. It consequently subjects us to far greater burdens and labors, dangers and temptations, while it brings with it an inconsiderable reward, and very little gratitude in the world. But Christ himself will be our reward, if we labor with fidelity. May He grant such mercy unto us who is the Father of all grace, to whom be given thanks and praises through Christ, our Lord, for ever! Amen.

WITTENBERG, A.D. 1529.

THE SMALL CATECHISM

PART I.
THE TEN COMMANDMENTS.
In the plain form in which they are to be taught by the head of a family.
THE FIRST COMMANDMENT.

I am the Lord thy God. Thou shalt have no other gods before Me.

[Thou shalt not make unto thee any graven image or any likeness of anything that is in heaven above, or that is in the earth beneath, or that is in the water under the earth; thou shalt not bow down thyself to them, nor serve them; for I the Lord thy God am a jealous God, visiting the iniquity of the fathers upon the children unto the third and fourth generation of them that hate Me; and showing mercy unto thousands of them that love Me, and keep my commandments.]

What is meant by this Commandment?

Answer. We should fear, love, and trust in God above all things.

THE SECOND COMMANDMENT.

Thou shalt not take the Name of the Lord thy God in vain; for the Lord will not hold him guiltless that taketh His Name in vain.

What is meant by this Commandment?

Ans. We should so fear and love God as not to curse, swear, conjure, lie, or deceive, by His Name, but call upon Him in every time of need, and worship Him with prayer, praise, and thanksgiving.

THE THIRD COMMANDMENT.

Remember the Sabbath-day, to keep it holy.

[Six days shalt thou labor, and do all thy work; but the seventh day is the Sabbath of the Lord thy God: in it thou shalt not do any work, thou, nor thy son, nor thy daughter, thy man-servant, nor thy maid-servant, nor thy cattle, nor thy stranger that is within thy gates: for in six days the Lord made heaven and earth, the sea, and all that in them is, and rested the seventh day; wherefore the Lord blessed the Sabbath day, and hallowed it.]

What is meant by this Commandment?

Ans. We should so fear and love God as not to despise His Word and the preaching of the Gospel, but deem it holy, and willing to hear and learn it.

THE FOURTH COMMANDMENT.

Honor thy father and thy mother, that thy days may be long upon the land which the Lord thy God giveth thee.

What is meant by this Commandment?

Ans. We should so fear and love God as not to despise nor displease our parents and superiors, but honor, serve, obey, love, and esteem them.

THE FIFTH COMMANDMENT.
Thou shalt not kill.
What is meant by this Commandment?
Ans. We should so fear and love God as not to do our neighbor any bodily harm or injury, but rather assist and comfort him in danger and want.

THE SIXTH COMMANDMENT.
Thou shalt not commit adultery.
What is meant by this Commandment?
Ans. We should so fear and love God as to be chaste and pure in our words and deeds, each one also loving and honoring his wife or her husband.

THE SEVENTH COMMANDMENT.
Thou shalt not steal.
What is meant by this Commandment?
Ans. We should so fear and love God as not to rob our neighbor of his money or property, nor bring it into our possession by unfair dealing or fraudulent means, but rather assist him to improve and protect it.

THE EIGHTH COMMANDMENT.
Thou shalt not bear false witness against thy neighbor.
What is meant by this Commandment?
Ans. We should so fear and love God as not deceitfully to belie, betray, slander, nor raise injurious reports against our neighbor, but apologize for him, speak well of him, and put the most charitable construction on all his actions.

THE NINTH COMMANDMENT.
Thou shalt not covet thy neighbor's house.
What is meant by this Commandment?
Ans. We should so fear and love God as not to desire by craftiness to gain possession of our neighbor's inheritance or home, or to obtain it under the pretext of a legal right, but be ready to assist and serve him in the preservation of his own.

THE TENTH COMMANDMENT.
Thou shalt not covet thy neighbor's wife, nor his manservant, nor his maid-servant, nor his ox, nor his ass, nor anything that is thy neighbor's.
What is meant by this Commandment?
Ans. We should so fear and love God as not to alienate our neighbor's wife from him, entice away his servants, nor let loose his cattle, but use our endeavors that they may remain and discharge their duty to him.

What does God declare concerning all these Commandments?
Ans. He says: I the Lord thy God am a jealous God, visiting the iniquity of the fathers upon the children unto the third and fourth generation of them that hate Me; and showing mercy unto thousands of them that love Me and keep my commandments.

What is meant by this declaration?
Ans. God threatens to punish all those who transgress these commandments. We should, therefore, dread His displeasure, and not act contrarily to these commandments. But He promises grace and every blessing to all who keep them. We should, therefore, love and trust in Him, and cheerfully do what He has commanded us.

PART II.
THE CREED.
In the plain form in which it is to be taught by the head of a family.
FIRST ARTICLE.—OF CREATION.

I believe in God the Father Almighty, Maker of heaven and earth.
What is meant by this Article?

Ans. I believe that God has created me and all that exists; that He has given and still preserves to me my body and soul with all my limbs and senses, my reason and all the faculties of my mind, together with my raiment, food, home, and family, and all my property; that He daily provides me abundantly with all the necessaries of life, protects me from all danger, and preserves me and guards me against all evil; all which He does out of pure, paternal, and divine goodness and mercy, without any merit or worthiness in me; for all which I am in duty bound to thank, praise, serve, and obey Him. This is most certainly true.

SECOND ARTICLE.—OF REDEMPTION.

And in Jesus Christ His only Son, our Lord; who was conceived by the Holy Ghost, born of the Virgin Mary; suffered under Pontius Pilate, was crucified, dead, and buried; He descended into hell; the third day He rose again from the dead; He ascended into heaven, and sitteth on the right hand of God the Father Almighty; from thence He shall come to judge the quick and the dead.

What is meant by this Article?

Ans. I believe that Jesus Christ, true God, begotten of the Father from eternity, and also true man, born of the Virgin Mary, is my Lord; who has redeemed me, a lost and condemned creature, secured and delivered me from all sins, from death, and from the power of the devil, not with silver and gold, but with His holy and precious blood, and with His innocent sufferings and death; in order that I might be His, live under Him in His kingdom, and serve Him in everlasting righteousness, innocence, and blessedness; even as He is risen from the dead, and lives and reigns to all eternity. This is most certainly true.

THIRD ARTICLE.—OF SANCTIFICATION.

I believe in the Holy Ghost; the holy Christian Church, the Communion of Saints; the Forgiveness of sins; the Resurrection of the body; and the Life everlasting. Amen.

What is meant by this Article?

Ans. I believe that I cannot by my own reason or strength believe in Jesus Christ my Lord, or come to Him; but the Holy Ghost has called me through the Gospel, enlightened me by His gifts, and sanctified and preserved me in the true faith; in like manner as He calls, gathers, enlightens, and sanctifies the whole Christian Church on earth, and preserves it in union with Jesus Christ in the true faith; in which Christian Church He daily forgives abundantly all my sins, and the sins of all believers, and will raise up me and all the dead at the last day, and will grant everlasting life to me and to all who believe in Christ. This is most certainly true.

PART III.
THE LORD'S PRAYER.

In the plain form in which it is to be taught by the head of a family.

INTRODUCTION.

Our Father Who art in heaven.

What is meant by this Introduction?

Ans. God would thereby affectionately encourage us to believe that He is truly our Father, and that we are His children indeed, so that we may call upon Him with all cheerfulness and confidence, even as beloved children entreat their affectionate parent.

FIRST PETITION.

Hallowed be Thy Name.

What is meant by this Petition?

Ans. The Name of God is indeed holy in itself; but we pray in this petition that it may be hallowed also by us.

How is this effected?

Ans. When the Word of God is taught in its truth and purity, and we, as the children of God, lead holy lives, in accordance with it; to this may our blessed Father in heaven help us! But whoever teaches and lives otherwise than as God's Word prescribes, profanes the Name of God among us; from this preserve us, Heavenly Father!

SECOND PETITION.

Thy kingdom come.

What is meant by this Petition?

Ans. The kingdom of God comes indeed of itself, without our prayer; but we pray in this petition that it may come unto us also.

When is this effected?

Ans. When our Heavenly Father gives us His Holy Spirit, so that by His grace we believe His holy Word, and live a godly life here on earth, and in heaven for ever.

THIRD PETITION.

Thy will be done on earth, as it is in heaven.

What is meant by this Petition?

Ans. The good and gracious will of God is done indeed without our prayer; but we pray in this petition that it may be done by us also.

When is this effected?

Ans. When God frustrates and brings to naught every evil counsel and purpose, which would hinder us from hallowing the Name of God, and prevent His kingdom from coming to us, such as the will of the devil, of the world, and of our own flesh; and when He strengthens us, and keeps us steadfast in His Word, and in the faith, even unto our end. This is His gracious and good will.

FOURTH PETITION.

Give us this day our daily bread.

What is meant by this Petition?

Ans. God gives indeed without our prayer even to the wicked also their daily bread; but we pray in this petition that He would make us sensible of His benefits, and enable us to receive our daily bread with thanksgiving.

What is implied in the words: "Our daily bread"?

Ans. All things that pertain to the wants and the support of this present life; such as food, raiment, money, goods, house and land, and other property; a believing spouse and good children; trustworthy servants and faithful magistrates; favorable seasons, peace and health; education and honor; true friends, good neighbors, and the like.

FIFTH PETITION.

And forgive us our trespasses, as we forgive those who trespass against us.

What is meant by this Petition?

Ans. We pray in this petition, that our Heavenly Father would not regard our sins, nor deny us our requests on account of them; for we are not worthy of anything for which we pray, and have not merited it; but that He would grant us all things through grace, although we daily commit much sin, and deserve chastisement alone. We will therefore, on our part, both heartily forgive, and also readily do good to those who may injure or offend us.

SIXTH PETITION.

And, lead us not into temptation.

What is meant by this Petition?

Ans. God indeed tempts no one to sin; but we pray in this petition that God would so guard and preserve us, that the devil, the world, and our own flesh, may not deceive us, nor lead us into error and unbelief, despair, and other great and shameful sins; and that, though we may be thus tempted, we may, nevertheless, finally prevail and gain the victory.

SEVENTH PETITION.

But deliver us from evil.
What is meant by this Petition?

Ans. We pray in this petition, as in a summary, that our Heavenly Father would deliver us from all manner of evil, whether it affect the body or soul, property or character, and, at last, when the hour of death shall arrive, grant us a happy end, and graciously take as from this world of sorrow to Himself in heaven.

CONCLUSION.

For Thine is the kingdom, and the power, and the glory, for ever and ever. Amen.
What is meant by the word "Amen"?

Ans. That I should be assured that such petitions are acceptable to our Heavenly Father, and are heard by Him; for He Himself has commanded us to pray in this manner, and has promised that He will hear us. Amen, Amen, that is, Yea, yea, it shall be so.

PART IV.
THE SACRAMENT OF HOLY BAPTISM.
In the plain form in which it is to be taught by the head of a family.

I. *What is Baptism?*

Ans. Baptism is not simply water, but it is the water comprehended in God's command, and connected with God's Word.

What is that Word of God?

Ans. It is that which our Lord Jesus Christ spoke, as it is recorded in the last chapter of Matthew, verse 19: "Go ye, and teach all nations, baptizing them in the Name of the Father, and of the Son, and of the Holy Ghost."

II. *What gifts or benefits does Baptism confer?*

Ans. It works forgiveness of sins, delivers from death and the devil, and confers everlasting salvation on all who believe, as the Word and promise of God declare.

What are such words and promises of God?

Ans. Those which our Lord Jesus Christ spoke, as they are recorded in the last chapter of Mark, verse 16: "He that believeth and is baptized, shall be saved; but he that believeth not, shall be damned."

III. *How can water produce such great effects?*

Ans. It is not the water indeed that produces these effects, but the Word of God which accompanies and is connected with the water, and our faith, which relies on the Word of God connected with the water. For the water, without the Word of God, is simply water and no baptism. But when connected with the Word of God, it is a baptism, that is, a gracious water of life, and a "washing of regeneration" in the Holy Ghost; as St. Paul says to Titus, in the third chapter, verses 5-8: "According to His mercy He saved us, by the washing of regeneration, and renewing of the Holy Ghost; which He shed on us abundantly through Jesus Christ our Saviour; that being justified by His grace, we should be made heirs according to the hope of eternal life. This is a faithful saying."

IV. *What does such baptizing with water signify?*

Ans. It signifies that the old Adam in us is to be drowned, and destroyed by daily sorrow and repentance, together with all sins and evil lusts; and that again, the new man should daily come forth and rise, that shall live in the presence of God in righteousness and purity forever.

Where is it so written?

Ans. St. Paul, in the Epistle to the Romans, chapter 6, verse 4, says: "We are buried with Christ by Baptism into death; that like as He was raised up from the dead by the glory of the Father, even so we also should walk in newness of life."

OF CONFESSION

What is Confession?

Ans. Confession consists of two parts: the one is, that we confess our sins; the other, that we receive absolution or forgiveness through the pastor as of God himself, in no wise doubting, but firmly believing that our sins are thus forgiven before God in heaven.

What sins ought we to confess?

Ans. In the presence of God we should acknowledge ourselves guilty of all manner of sins, even of those which we do not ourselves perceive; as we do in the Lord's Prayer. But in the presence of the pastor we should confess those sins alone of which we have knowledge, and which we feel in our hearts.

Which are these?

Ans. Here reflect on your condition, according to the Ten Commandments, namely: Whether you are a father or mother, a son or daughter, a master or mistress, a manservant or maidservant—whether you have been disobedient, unfaithful, slothful—whether you have injured any one by words or actions-whether you have stolen, neglected, or wasted aught, or done other evil.

PART V.
THE SACRAMENT OF THE ALTAR,
OR, THE LORD'S SUPPER.

In the plain form in which it is to be taught by the head of a family.

What is the Sacrament of the Altar?

Ans. It is the true Body and Blood of our Lord Jesus Christ, under the bread and wine, given unto us Christians to eat and to drink, as it was instituted by Christ Himself.

Where is it so written?

Ans. The Holy Evangelists, Matthew, Mark, and Luke, together with St. Paul, write thus:

"Our Lord Jesus Christ, the same night in which He was betrayed, took bread: and when He had given thanks, He brake it, and gave it to His disciples, and said, Take, eat; this is my Body, which is given for you: this do, in remembrance of Me.

"After the same manner also He took the cup, when He had supped, gave thanks, and gave it to them, saying, Drink ye all of it: this cup is the new testament in my Blood, which is shed for you, for the remission of sins: this do, as oft as ye drink it, in remembrance of Me."

What benefits are derived from such eating and drinking?

Ans. They are pointed out in these words; "given and shed for you, for the remission of sins." Namely, through these words, the remission of sins, life and salvation are granted unto us in the Sacrament. For where there is remission of sins, there are also life and salvation.

How can the bodily eating and drinking produce such great effects?

Ans. The eating and the drinking, indeed, do not produce them, but the words which stand here, namely: "given, and shed for you, for the remission of sins." These words are, besides the bodily eating and drinking, the chief things in the Sacrament; and he who believes these words, has that which they declare and set forth, namely, the remission of sins.

Who is it, then, that receives this Sacrament worthily?

Ans. Fasting and bodily preparation are indeed a good external discipline; but he is truly worthy and well prepared who believes these words, "given and shed for you, for the remission of sins." But he who does not believe these words, or who doubts, is unworthy and unfit: for the words: "FOR YOU," require truly believing hearts.

MORNING AND EVENING PRAYER.
In the plain form in which it is to be taught by the head of a family.
MORNING.
In the Morning, when thou risest, thou shalt say:
In the Name of the Father, and of the Son, and of the Holy Ghost, Amen.

Then, kneeling or standing, thou shalt say the Apostles' Creed *and the* Lord's Prayer.

Then mayest than say this Prayer:
I give thanks unto Thee, Heavenly Father, through Jesus Christ Thy dear Son, that Thou hast protected me through the night from all danger and harm; and I beseech Thee to preserve and keep me this day also, from all sin and evil; that in all my thoughts, words, and deeds, I may serve and please Thee. Into Thy hands I commend my body and soul, and all that is mine. Let Thy holy angel have charge concerning me, that the wicked one may have no power over me. Amen.

And then shouldst thou go with joy to thy work, after a Hymn, or the Ten Commandments, *or whatever thy devotion may suggest.*

EVENING.
In the Evening, when thou goest to bed, thou shall say:
In the Name of the Father, and of the Son, and of the Holy Ghost. Amen.

Then, kneeling or standing, thou shalt say the Apostles' Creed *and the* Lord's Prayer.

Then mayest thou say this Prayer:
I give thanks unto Thee, Heavenly Father, through Jesus Christ Thy dear Son, that Thou hast this day so graciously protected me, and I beseech Thee to forgive me all my sins, and the wrong which I have done, and by Thy great mercy defend me from all the perils and dangers of this night. Into thy hands I commend my body and soul, and all that is mine. Let Thy holy angel have charge concerning me, that the wicked one may have no power over me. Amen.

And then lie down, in peace, and sleep.

BLESSING AND THANKSGIVING AT TABLE.
In the plain form in which they are to be taught by the head of a family.
BEFORE MEAT.
Before meat, the members of the family surrounding the table reverently and with folded hands, there shall be said:
The eyes of all wait upon Thee, O Lord: and Thou givest them their meat in due season. Thou openest Thine hand, and satisfiest the desire of every living thing.

Then shall be said the Lord's Prayer, *and after that this* Prayer:
O Lord God, Heavenly Father, bless unto us these Thy gifts, which of Thy tender kindness Thou hast bestowed upon us, through Jesus Christ our Lord. Amen.

After meat, reverently and with folded hands, there shall be said:
O give thanks unto the Lord, for He is good: for His mercy endureth for ever. He giveth food to all flesh; He giveth to the beast his food, and to the young ravens which cry. The Lord taketh pleasure in them that tear Him; in those that hope in His mercy,

Then shall be said the Lord's Prayer, *and after that this* Prayer:
We give thanks, to Thee, O God. Our Father, for all Thy benefits, through Jesus Christ our Lord, Who with Thee liveth and reigneth, for ever and ever. Amen.

TABLE OF DUTIES.
Or, certain passages of the Scriptures, selected for various orders and conditions of men, wherein their respective duties are set forth.
BISHOPS, PASTORS, AND PREACHERS.
A bishop must be blameless, the husband of one wife, vigilant, sober, of good behavior, given to hospitality, apt to teach; not given to wine, no striker, not greedy of

filthy lucre: but patient, not a brawler, not covetous; one that ruleth well his own house, having his children in subjection with all gravity; not a novice, but holding fast the faithful word as he hath been taught, that he may be able by sound doctrine both to exhort and to convince the gainsayers.—I Tim. 3:2-6; Tit. 1:9.

WHAT DUTIES HEARERS OWE THEIR BISHOPS.

Even so hath the Lord ordained that they which preach the Gospel should live of the Gospel.—[I Cor. 9:14.] Let him that is taught in the Word communicate unto him that teacheth in all good things,—Gal. 6:6. Let the elders that rule well be counted worthy of double honor, especially they who labor in word and doctrine. For the Scripture saith, Thou shalt not muzzle the ox that treadeth out the corn. And, The laborer is worthy of his reward.—I Tim. 5:17, 18. Obey them that have the rule over you, and submit yourselves; for they watch for your souls, as they that must give account, that they may do it with joy and not with grief; for that is unprofitable for you.—Heb. 13:17.

MAGISTRATES.

Let every soul be subject unto the higher powers. For there is no power but of God; the powers that be are ordained of God; for rulers are not a terror to good works, but to the evil. Wilt thou then not be afraid of the power? do that which is good, and thou shall have praise of the same; for he is the minister of God to thee for good. But if thou do that which is evil, be afraid; for he beareth not the sword in vain: for he is the minister of God, a revenger to execute wrath upon him that doeth evil.—Rom. 13:1-4.

WHAT DUTIES SUBJECTS OWE MAGISTRATES.

Render therefore unto Caesar the things that are Caesar's.—Matt. 22:21. Let every soul be subject unto the higher powers, etc. Wherefore we must needs be subject, not only for wrath, but also for conscience' sake. For this cause pay ye tribute also; for they are God's ministers, attending continually upon this very thing. Render therefore to all their dues; tribute to whom tribute is due; custom to whom custom; fear to whom fear; honor to whom honor.—Rom. 13:1, 5. I exhort, therefore, that, first of all, supplications, prayers, intercessions, and giving of thanks be made for all men; for kings and for all that are in authority, that we may lead a quiet and peaceable life in all godliness and honesty.—I Tim. 2. Put them in mind to be subject to principalities and powers, etc.—Tit. 3:1. Submit yourselves to every ordinance of man for the Lord's sake: whether it be to the king as supreme; or unto governors as unto them that are sent, etc.—I Pet. 2:13.

HUSBANDS.

Ye husbands, dwell with your wives according to knowledge, giving honor unto the wife, as unto the weaker vessel, and as being heirs together of the grace of life; that your prayers be not hindered.—1 Pet. 3:7. And be not bitter against them.—Col. 3:19.

WIVES.

Wives submit yourselves unto your husbands, as unto the Lord—even as Sarah obeyed Abraham, calling him lord; whose daughters ye are, as long as ye do well, and are not afraid with any amazement.—Eph. 5:22; I Pet. 3:6.

PARENTS.

Ye fathers, provoke not your children to wrath: but bring them up in the nurture and admonition of the Lord.—Eph. 6:4.

CHILDREN.

Children, obey your parents in the Lord: for this is right. Honor thy father and thy mother; which is the first commandment with promise; that it may be well with thee, and thou mayest live long on the earth.—Eph. 6:1-3.

MALE AND FEMALE SERVANTS AND LABORERS.

Servants, be obedient to them that are your masters according to the flesh, with fear and trembling, in singleness of your heart, as unto Christ; not with eye-service, as men-pleasers; but as the servants of Christ doing the will of God from the heart; with good will doing service as to the Lord, and not to men; knowing that whatsoever good thing any man doeth, the same shall he receive of the Lord, whether he be bond or free.—Eph. 6:5-8

MASTERS AND MISTRESSES.
Ye masters, do the same things unto them, forbearing threatening; knowing that your Master also is in heaven; neither is there respect of persons with Him.—Eph. 6:9

YOUNG PERSONS IN GENERAL.
Likewise, ye younger, submit yourselves unto the elder. Yea, all of you be subject one to another, and be clothed with humility: for God resisteth the proud, and giveth grace to the humble. Humble yourselves therefore under the mighty hand of God, that He may exalt you in due time.—I Pet. 5:5, 6.

WIDOWS.
She that is a widow indeed, and desolate, trusteth in God, and continueth in supplications and prayers night and day; but she that liveth in pleasure is dead while she liveth.—I Tim. 5:5, 6.

CHRISTIANS IN GENERAL.
Thou shall love thy neighbor as thyself. Herein are comprehended all the commandments.—Rom. 13:9, 10. And persevere in prayer for all men.—I Tim. 2:1, 2.

AN EXPLANATION
OF
LUTHER'S SMALL CATECHISM

CHAPTER I.
THE BIBLE.

THE BIBLE is the inspired and unerring record of what God has revealed to men concerning Himself and the Way of Salvation. [II Tim. 3:16+, Gal. 1:8] Hence, if we ask, "What must I do to be saved?" the answer to our question must be sought in the Bible. It tells us what to believe and what to do in order that we may belong to God's kingdom on earth and in heaven. [Matt. 6:33+, Acts 16:30+, John 5:39+] It is the only rule and standard of Christian faith and life.

WHY NEEDED. Even without the Bible, men know that there is a Higher Being. Their own conscience tells them that there is a God who will punish them if they do wrong; [Rom 2:14, 15] and the works of nature proclaim that there is an Almighty Being who created them. [Ps. 19:1+] But the knowledge of God which men gain from their own conscience and from nature is insufficient. Neither nature nor conscience can tell us anything about the Way of Salvation which God has prepared for us in Jesus Christ. It is only from the Bible that we can learn how we shall be saved.

ITS INSPIRATION. The Bible is the Word of God. It was written by holy men whom God inspired. [II Pet. 1:21+] It contains knowledge which no man could have discovered by his own power. It foretells events which no uninspired man could have foreseen. It contains teachings so exalted and holy that they could not have originated in the heart of man. It possesses a power such as no merely human book ever did or could possess. [Heb. 4:12]

ITS OBJECT is to make us wise unto salvation. [II Tim. 3:15+, Prov 9:10+] It is to be a lamp unto our feet and a light unto our path [Ps. 119:105+] to guide us safely through this world to our heavenly home. It contains all that we need to know and all that we ever shall know in this world concerning God and His will. [Luke: 6:31] It is the final and absolute authority in all matters of religion. We should, therefore, pay most earnest heed to its teachings, believe them with all our heart, and apply them in our lives.

ITS CONTENTS. It consists of sixty-six "books," written between the years 1500 B.C. and 100 A.D., and contains the History and the Doctrines of the Kingdom of God.

OLD AND NEW TESTAMENTS. The Bible consists of two parts: The Old Testament and the New Testament, The Old Testament reaches from Creation to about 400 B.C., and shows how God prepared the world for Christ's kingdom. The New Testament reaches from the birth of Christ to the end of the world, and shows how Christ came and established His kingdom.

LAW AND GOSPEL. The Bible contains Law, [Micah 6:8+] telling us what we must do, and Gospel, [John 3:16+] telling us how we are to be saved. The Old Testament contains principally Law, and the New Testament contains principally Gospel. But there are Law and Gospel in both. The Gospel in the Old Testament is prophetical. The Old Testament prepared the way for the New; the New Testament is the fulfilment of the Old. With the New Testament, God's revelation to men was completed; [Heb. 1:1, 2+, Heb. 2:1-3] no further revelation will be given.

THE BOOKS OF THE OLD TESTAMENT.

Historical.

Genesis, Exodus, Leviticus, Numbers, Deuteronomy, Joshua, Judges, Ruth, I Samuel, II Samuel, I Kings, II Kings, I Chronicles, II Chronicles, Ezra, Nehemiah, Esther.

Poetical.

Job, Psalms, Proverbs, Ecclesiastes, Song of Solomon.

Prophetical.

Isaiah, Jeremiah, Lamentations, Ezekiel, Daniel, Hosea, Joel, Amos, Obadiah, Jonah, Micah, Nahum, Habakkuk, Zephaniah, Haggai, Zechariah, Malachi.

The *historical* books of the Old Testament give an account of the creation of the world and of man, of the entrance of sin and death, of God's covenant with Israel to save them, and of the history of Israel as God's chosen people. The *poetical* books give the teachings of the Old Testament covenant in prayers, proverbs and hymns. The*prophetical* books contain many instructions, admonitions and prophecies (especially concerning Christ who should come to save men) which God sent to the Israelites through the prophets. The first four prophets are called the Major Prophets; and the last twelve, the Minor Prophets.

THE BOOKS OF THE NEW TESTAMENT.

Historical.

Matthew, Mark, Luke, John, Acts.

Didactical.

Romans, I Corinthians, II Corinthians, Galatians, Ephesians, Philippians, Colossians, I Thessalonians, II Thessalonians, I Timothy, II Timothy, Titus, Philemon, Hebrews, James, I Peter, II Peter, I John, II John, III John, Jude

Prophetical.

Revelation.

The *historical* books of the New Testament give an account of the life of our Lord Jesus Christ and of some of His apostles. The *didactical* books (the epistles or letters) explain the Gospel of Christ more fully, and show how we are to believe in Him aright and live aright. The *prophetical* book tells in figurative language what shall take place in the Church of Christ up to the time when there shall be new heavens and a new earth.

CANONICAL BOOKS. The sixty-six books enumerated above are inspired, and are called the Canonical Books of the Old and New Testaments. The so-called Apocryphal Books, printed in some editions of the Bible, are not a part of the Bible: they are not inspired.

OUR ENGLISH BIBLE. The Old Testament was originally written in Hebrew, and the New Testament in Greek. Our English Bible is a translation from the Hebrew and the Greek. The English Bible which is in ordinary use is called the Authorized Version, or King James' Version. It is a translation made by a body of learned men and published in England in 1611, during the reign of James I. The Revised Version is an improved translation made by a body of learned men in England and America and published in 1881-1885. The Bible in whole or in part has been translated into more than three hundred languages.

QUESTIONS.—1. What is the Bible? 2. What does it tell us? 3. Why do we need it? 4. Why do we say that the Bible is the Word of God? 5. What is its object? 6. What does it contain? 7. Of what two parts does the Bible consist, and how far do they reach? 8. What do we mean by Law and Gospel, and where are they found? 9. What is the relation between the Old and New Testaments? 10. Name the books of the Old Testament. 11. What do the historical, poetical and prophetical books of the Old Testament contain. 12. Name the books of the New Testament. 13. What do the historical, didactical and prophetical books of the New Testament contain? 14. How many canonical books of the Bible are there? 15. In what languages was the Bible originally written? 16. Tell what you know about the English Bible? 17. Into how many languages has the Bible in whole or in part been translated?

SCRIPTURE VERSES.—II Tim. 3:16, 17. All Scripture is given by inspiration of God, and is profitable for doctrine, for reproof, for correction, for instruction in righteousness: that the man of God may be perfect, thoroughly furnished unto all good works.

Matt. 6:33. Seek ye first the kingdom of God, and his righteousness; and all these things shall be added unto you.

Acts 16:30, 31. What must I do to be saved? And they said, Believe on the Lord Jesus Christ, and thou shalt be saved, and thy house.

John 5:39. Search the Scriptures: for in them ye think ye have eternal life: and they are they which testify of me.

Ps. 19:1. The heavens declare the glory of God, and the firmament showeth his handiwork.

II Pet. 1:21. For the prophecy came not in old time by the will of man: but holy men of God spake as they were moved by the Holy Ghost.

II Tim. 3:15. From a child thou hast known the holy scriptures, which are able to make thee wise unto salvation through faith which is in Christ Jesus.

Prov. 9:10. The fear of the Lord is the beginning of wisdom.

Ps. 119:105. Thy word is a lamp unto my feet, and a light unto my path.

Micah 6:8. He hath showed thee, O man, what is good; and what doth the Lord require of thee, but to do justly, to love mercy, and to walk humbly with thy God.

John 3:16. God so loved the world, that he gave his only begotten Son, that whosoever believeth in him should not perish, but have everlasting life.

Heb. 1:1, 2. God, who at sundry times and in divers manners spake in time past unto the fathers by the prophets, hath in these last days spoken unto us by his Son, whom he hath appointed heir of all things, by whom also he made the worlds.

READING.—The Child Jesus in the Temple, Luke 2:41-52; or Mary sitting at Jesus' Feet, Luke 10:38-42.

ILLUSTRATIONS.—*Study of the Scriptures:* Jesus and the Apostles at home in them, Matt. 4:4-10, Acts 2: 14*seq.* Timothy, II Tim. 3:15. The Bereans, Acts 17:10-12. *Variously received:* The Parable of the Sower, Luke 8:5-15.

CHAPTER II.
THE CATECHISM.

The object of catechetical instruction is to fit us for communicant membership in the Church. Those who were baptized in infancy are members of the Church; but they are not admitted to the Lord's Supper, and hence do not become communicant members, until they have been instructed and confirmed.

Luther's Small Catechism is our text-book for catechetical instruction. It is not only the best book for this purpose, but is one of the Confessions of our Church, and should become our personal confession of faith, it is called Luther's *Small* Catechism, because Luther wrote a larger one also.

THE AUTHOR of our catechism was Dr. Martin Luther (b. 1483, d. 1546), the great Reformer, through whom God effected the Reformation of the Church, in the sixteenth century. He began the Reformation with his Ninety-five Theses against the sale of indulgences, contended against the many errors and abuses that had crept into the Church, and preached and taught the pure truth of the Gospel, until his death. (Ninety-five Theses, 1517; Translation of the Bible into German, 1522-34; Larger and Smaller Catechisms, 1529; Augsburg Confession adopted 1530.)

THE CATECHISM Contains the principal teachings of the Bible,—those things which we need to know in order to be saved and to lead a right Christian life. [Acts 16:30, Matt. 6:33] It is not meant to displace the Bible, but to fit us to read and study the Bible with greater profit. [John 5:39]

THE FIVE PRINCIPAL PARTS of the catechism are 1. The Ten Commandments. 2. The Creed. 3. The Lord's Prayer. 4. The Sacrament of Holy Baptism. 5. The Sacrament of the Altar[1]. To these are added Questions on Confession, Morning and Evening Prayers, Thanksgiving before and after Meat, and A Table of Duties.

[Footnote 1: Luther says that three things are necessary for every one who would be saved. Like a sick person, 1. He must know what his sickness is. 2. He must know where the medicine is which will cure him. 3. He must desire and seek the medicine, and have it brought to him. Our sickness (sin) is revealed to us by the Ten Commandments. The medicine (God's grace) is made known to us in the Creed. We seek and ask for it in the Lord's Prayer. It is brought to us in the Sacraments.]

QUESTIONS.—1. What is the object of catechetical instruction? 2. What is to be said about the relation of baptized children to the Church? 3. What is Luther's Small Catechism, and what should it become for us? 4. Who was the author of our Catechism? 5. What does our Catechism contain? 6. Name the five principal parts of the catechism, and the additions to them.

SCRIPTURE READING.—Paul confesses his Faith, Acts 26.

PART I.
THE TEN COMMANDMENTS.

CHAPTER III.
THE LAW.

The Ten Commandments are called the *Moral Law*, or more briefly the Law, and sometimes the Decalogue or the Ten Words. They make known to us God's will, which is the law for all His creatures. Each commandment has a *negative* side, and *forbids* something; each has also a *positive* side, and *commands* or enjoins something.

The Giving Of The Law. The Law of God was originally written in man's heart at creation. [Rom. 2:15] We call that law in the heart, Conscience. After the fall into sin, the conscience became darkened, and men did not always know right from wrong, and fell into gross idolatry. [Rom. 1:21-23] God, therefore, through Moses at Mount Sinai, gave men His law anew, [Exod. 20:1] written on two Tables of stone. [Exod. 31:18] He also gave the Israelites national and ceremonial laws. These, being meant for a particular people and a certain era of the world, are no longer binding upon us. But the Moral Law has been expressly confirmed by our Lord Jesus Christ as valid for all time and binding upon all men. [Matt. 22:37-40+]

The substance of the law is, "Thou shalt love the Lord Thy God with all thy heart and with all thy soul and with all thy mind." and "Thou shalt love thy neighbor as thyself."

The purpose of the law is, 1. To put a check upon wicked men, [I Tim. 1:9] 2. To convince us of our sinfulness [Rom. 3:20+] and our need of the Saviour, [Gal. 3:24+] and 3. To be our rule and guide for Christian conduct. [John. 14:15+, Matt. 7:12+] It is especially with respect to the second purpose here mentioned, that the Ten Commandments were assigned by Luther to the first and not to a later place in his catechism.

The Two Tables. The Ten Commandments may be divided into two parts, called the Two Tables of the Law. [Exod. 31:18] The First Table includes the first three commandments, and teaches us our Duty to God. The Second Table Includes the last seven commandments, and teaches us our Duty to our Fellow-men.[2]

[Footnote 2: The Ten Commandments are not numbered in the Bible. A two-fold numbering is found among Christians. The first is that which is given in our Catechism, and which is accepted by the majority of Christians, The other numbering makes two commandments of our first (the second being the command not to make any images), and joins our ninth and tenth into one. This makes a difference in the numbering of all the commandments except the first.]

Questions.—1. What other names are given to the Tea Commandments? 2. What do they make known to us? 3. What two sides are there to each commandment? 4. Where was the law of God originally written? 5. Why and when was the Law given anew? 6. Why is the Moral Law binding upon us, while the national and ceremonial laws of Israel are not? 7. What is the substance of the Law? 8. What is the threefold purpose of the Law? 9. Into how many Tables is the Law divided, and what does each Table teach? 10. How many commandments does each Table include?

SCRIPTURE VERSES.—Matt. 22:37-40. Jesus said unto him, Thou shall love the Lord thy God with all thy heart, and with all thy soul, and with all thy mind. This is the first and great commandment. And the second is like unto it, Thou shalt love thy neighbour as thyself. On these two commandments hang all the law and the prophets.

Rom. 3:20. Therefore by the deeds of the law there shall no flesh be justified in his sight: for by the law is the knowledge of sin.

Gal. 3:24. Wherefore the law was our schoolmaster to bring us unto Christ, that we might be justified by faith.

John 14:15. If ye love me, keep my commandments.

Matt. 7:12. Therefore all things whatsoever ye would that men should do to you, do ye even so to them: for this is the law and the prophets.

Reading.—The Giving of the Law at Mt. Sinai, Exod. 19 and 20.

CHAPTER IV.
THE LAWGIVER.

I am the Lord thy God.

These introductory words show who is the Lawgiver. [Jas. 4:12] As earthly kings place their names at the beginning of their decrees to give them authority, so God places

His name at the beginning of the commandments in order to make known who gives them, and whose displeasure we shall incur if we disobey them. These introductory words belong not only to the first but to all the commandments.

I AM. By these words God reminds us that He is a Person. He speaks to us. He is not an impersonal God who pervades and is a part of nature. He is above nature and has created it. [Gen 1:1]

THE LORD. The word here translated "Lord" means in the original Hebrew "I AM THAT I AM." [Exod 8:14+] God thereby declares that He is the One and Only Self-existent, [Isa 44:6+] Eternal, [Ps 90:1, 2+] and Unchangeable Being. [Mal 3:6+] He is the true and living God in contradistinction from all so-called gods. [Jer 10:10] The name Jehovah or "LORD" is used in the Old Testament Scriptures to designate God as the covenant God of Israel. It signified that He stood in a specially near relation to them as His chosen people. The name has the same comforting meaning for Christians; for they are the New Testament people of God. [Tit 2:14+, I Pet 2-9]

THY GOD. These words express God's good-will toward us. He is *our God* who loves [Jer 31:3+] us and cares for us. [I Pet 5:7] He said to Israel, "I am the Lord thy God, which brought thee out of the land of Egypt, out of the house of bondage." He has delivered *us* from the still greater bondage of sin, death, and the devil through His Son Jesus Christ, [Col 1:13+] and has a right to expect our gratitude and love.

THE LORD THY GOD. He who gives us these commandments is a Spirit [John 4:24+] of infinite majesty and goodness. He is:

1. *Eternal*; He always was and always will be. [Ps 90:2]

2. *Unchangeable*; He always was and always will be the same. [Mal 3:6]

3. *Omnipresent*; He is present everywhere at the same time and all the time. [Ps 139:7-11]

4. *Omniscient*; He knows all the past, present, and future, and is acquainted with every thought, desire, and purpose of our hearts. [Ps 139:2]

5. *Omnipotent*, or Almighty; He is able to do all things which He wills to do. [Luke 1:37]

6. *Holy*; He is perfectly pure, and separate from all that is evil. [Isa. 6:3]

7. *Just*; He will bless those who keep His law, and punish those who break it. [Rom. 2:6]

8. *All-wise*; He always knows what is the best thing to do, and the best way to do it. [Col. 2:3]

9. *Good*; He is Love itself. [I John 4:8] He is kind even to the unthankful, [Matt. 5:45] merciful to the penitent soul for Jesus' sake, [John 3:16] and longsuffering toward the impenitent in order to lead them to repentance by His goodness. [II Pet. 3:9, Rom. 2:4]

10. *Faithful and True*; He can be absolutely relied upon to do all that He has promised or threatened. [Numb. 23:19]

Because of the Majesty and Goodness of the Lord our God, we should FEAR and LOVE HIM, and KEEP His commandments.

QUESTIONS—1. What do the introductory words show? 2. Of what do the words "I am" remind us? 3. What is the meaning of the Hebrew word translated "Lord"? 4. What do the words "thy God" express? 5. From what bondage has God delivered us? 6. Name and define God's attributes? 7. Why should we fear and love God?

SCRIPTURE VERSES.—Exod. 3:14. And God said unto Moses, I AM THAT I AM.

Isa. 44:6. Thus saith the LORD the King of Israel, and his Redeemer the LORD of hosts; I am the first, and I am the last; and beside me there is no God.

Ps. 90:1, 2. LORD, thou hast been our dwelling place in all generations. Before the mountains were brought forth, or ever thou hadst formed the earth and the world, even from everlasting to everlasting, thou art God.

Mal. 3:6. For I am the LORD. I change not.

Tit. 2:14. Who gave himself for us, that he might redeem us from all iniquity, and purify unto himself a peculiar people, zealous of good works.

Jer. 31:3. I have loved thee with an everlasting love: therefore with lovingkindness have I drawn thee.

Col. 1:13, 14. Who hath delivered us from the power of darkness, and hath translated us into the kingdom of his dear Son: in whom we have redemption through his blood, even the forgiveness of sins.

John 4:24. God is a Spirit: and they that worship him must worship him in spirit and in truth.

READING.—Ps. 14: Ps. 121.

THE FIRST TABLE OF THE LAW.
OUR DUTY TO GOD.

"Thou shalt love the Lord thy God with all thy heart, and with all thy mind, and with all thy soul." [Matt. 22:37]

CHAPTER V.
THE FIRST COMMANDMENT
GOD.

Thou shalt have no other gods before me.
What is meant by this commandment?
We should fear, love and trust in God above all things.

THE GREAT COMMANDMENT. This is the great commandment of the Law, because it includes all the rest. [Matt. 22:37,38] Obedience to all the commandments must proceed from the love of God which the first commandment requires. [Rom. 13:9,10] Hence the explanation of the other nine begins with the words, "We should so fear and love God."

This Commandment *forbids* us to worship false gods, and *commands* us to worship the true God by fearing, loving and trusting in Him above all things.

I. WHAT IS FORBIDDEN.

1. ALL IDOLATRY. "Thou shalt have no other gods." Idolatry is committed by all who put anything in God's place, the highest place in the heart. "Whatever we set our heart upon is our god."

Open Idolatry [Exod. 32:1-9, Ps. 135:15-17, Isa. 42:8, Rom. 1:22-23] is committed by those who worship imaginary beings, the sun, moon, or stars, animals, dead ancestors, idols made with hands, images,[3] pictures, the Virgin Mary, saints, angels, the devil, or any other creature.

[Footnote 3: When God gave the commandments to Israel, He forbade them to make any graven images or likenesses. God being a Spirit, the making of an image of God would at that period necessarily have resulted in idolatry. But since Christ has come in the flesh and was visible among men, we are permitted to make pictures and images of Him. Luther preached very forcibly against those persons who, during his absence from Wittenberg, destroyed the pictures and images in the churches. He said that we make a picture of Christ in our heart whenever we think of Him, and put pictures of Him in the Bible and other books; and that therefore it is not wrong to place pictures or images of Him in our churches, so long as we do not worship them.]

Secret Idolatry is committed by all who put (a) Self, [Prov. 3:6, 6.+, Jer. 9:23, 24] (b) Fellow-men [Acts 5:29+, Matt. 10:28+, Matt. 10:37+, Ps. 146:3-5] or (c) Objects of this world [I John 2:15-17+] (money, fame, business, pleasure, etc.) above God, by fearing, loving, or trusting in them more than in God.

2. Godlessness. [Sam. 2:30, Ps. 10:4] Neglect to worship the true God, unbelief, scepticism, superstition, Infidelity, and atheism are a transgression of this commandment.

3. Double service. [Matt. 6:24+] God forbids us to have other gods before or besides Him, He demands our whole heart.

II. WHAT IS COMMANDED.

We should give God the highest place in our hearts, and "fear, love and trust in Him above all things." [Matt. 4:10+]

1. WE SHOULD FEAR GOD ABOVE ALL THINGS. We should be more afraid of His anger than of anything else in the whole world. [Gen. 39:9+, Ps. 33:8, 9.] Rather than disobey Him, we should be willing to suffer ridicule, persecution, loss of money, property, position, or friends, and even death itself. [Matt. 10:28+, Acts 5:29]

Why. We should fear God above all things, 1. Because He is omniscient, and we cannot hide anything from Him, not even our thoughts. [Ps. 139:1, 2+] 2. Because He is holy, and hates everything that is evil. [Lev. 19:2] 3. Because He is just, and will punish every sin. [Ps. 5:4]

How. As Christians, our fear of God should be a child-like and not a slavish fear. Child-like fear is fear mingled with love. We should refrain from evil not simply from fear of punishment, but from fear of offending the God whom we love. [Rom. 8:15+] "Slavish fear Is afraid God will come; child-like fear is afraid He will go away."

2. WE SHOULD LOVE GOD ABOVE ALL THINGS, "with all our heart, and with all our mind and with all our soul." [Matt. 22:37] Our first aim and our highest delight should always be to do God's will. [I John 5:3+] We should be far more anxious to please Him than to please ourselves or any of our fellow-men. We should love Him far more than we love any one else [Matt. 10:37+] (parents, brothers, sisters, friends, etc.), or any earthly objects [I John 2:15+] (money, pleasure, business and the like).

Why. We should love God above all things 1. Because He is most worthy of our love. [Ps. 73:25, 26+] 2. Because He first loved us, [I John 4:19+, I John 4:9+] and gave His Son to die for us. 3. Because our highest happiness is found in loving Him.

How we should show our Love. We should show that we love God above all things 1. By leading a godly life. [II John 6] 2. By loving the things of God, especially the Church and the Gospel. [John 8:47] 3. By loving our fellow-men for His sake. [I John 4:20+]

3. WE SHOULD TRUST IN GOD ABOVE ALL THINGS. We should rely with all our heart upon His love and care, [Prov. 3:5+] placing our chief dependence on Him, and not on our own wisdom, skill, or strength, or upon men, money etc.

Why. We should trust in God with all our heart because 1. He loves us. [Rom. 8:32] 2. He knows all our wants. [Matt. 6:32] 3. He knows what is best for us. 4. He is able to do all things. 5. He has promised to care for us. [Heb. 13:5, Isa. 54:10, Isa. 41:10]

How we should show our Trust. If we trust in God above all things we will show that trust, 1. By freedom from unbelieving care and worry. [Matt. 6:25, I Pet. 5:7+] 2. By reliance upon God's help and protection at all times. [Ps. 33:18, 19] 3. By committing the entire ordering of our lives to Him. [Ps. 37:5+]

We have all broken this first commandment; for we have not always and everywhere feared, loved and trusted in God above all things.

QUESTIONS—1. Why is this the Great Commandment? 2. Why does the explanation of all the other commandments begin with the words, "We should so fear and love God"? 3. What does this first commandment forbid? 4. What does it command? 5. What two kinds of Idolatry are there? 6. Mention some forms of open idolatry. 7. Mention some forms of secret idolatry. 8. What does it mean to fear God above all things? 9. Why should we fear him? 10. How should we fear Him? 11. What does it mean to love God above all things? 12. Why should we love God above all things? 13. How should we show our love to God? 14. What does it mean to trust in God above all things? 15. Why should we trust in God above all things? 16. How should we show our trust in God? 17. Have we kept this commandment?

SCRIPTURE VERSES.—Prov. 3:5, 6. Trust In the Lord with all thine heart, and lean not unto thine own understanding.

Acts 5:29. Then Peter and the other apostles answered and said, We ought to obey God rather than men.

Matt. 10:28, And fear not them which kill the body, but are not able to kill the soul; but rather fear him which is able to destroy both soul and body in hell.

Matt. 10:37. He that loveth father or mother more than me is not worthy of me: and he that loveth son or daughter more than me is not worthy of me.

1 John 2:15. Love not the world, neither the things that are in the world. If any man love the world, the love of the Father is not in him.

Matt. 6:24. No man can serve two masters: for either he will hate the one, and love the other; or else he will hold to the one, and despise the other. Ye cannot serve God and mammon.

Matt. 4:10. Thou shall worship the Lord thy God, and him only shalt thou serve.

Gen. 38:9. How then can I do this great wickedness, and sin against God?

Ps. 139:1, 2. O Lord, thou hast searched me, and known me. Thou knowest my downsitting and my uprising, thou understandest my thoughts afar off.

Rom. 8:15. For ye have not received the spirit of bondage again to fear; but ye have received the Spirit of adoption, whereby we cry, Abba, Father.

I John 5:3. For this is the love of God, that we keep his commandments: and his commandments are not grievous.

Ps. 73:25, 28. Whom have I in heaven but thee? and there is none upon earth that I desire beside thee. My flesh and my heart faileth; but God is the strength of my heart and my portion forever.

I John 4:19. We love him, because he first loved us.

I John 4:9. In this was manifested the love of God towards us, because that God sent his only begotten Son into the world, that we might live through him.

I John 4:20. If a man say, I love God, and hateth his brother, he is a liar; for he that loveth not his brother whom he hath seen, how can he love God whom he hath not seen?

I Pet. 5:7. Casting all your care upon him; for he careth for you.

Ps. 37:5. Commit thy way unto the Lord, trust also in him; and he shall bring it to pass.

READING.—The Golden Calf, Exod. 32; or, The Golden Image, Dan. 3.

ILLUSTRATIONS.—*Secret* Idolatry: Goliath, I Sam. 17:41 *seq*; Nebuchadnezzar, Dan. 4:25 *seq*.; Herod, Acts 12:21-23; The Rich Young Ruler, Matt. 19:16-22; The Rich Fool, Luke 12:15-21. *Slavish Fear*: Adam, Gen. 3:10-11. *Child-like Fear*: Joseph, Gen. 39:9. *Love to God*: Abraham, Gen. 22:1-14; Peter and John, Acts 4:19, 20; Jesus, John 4:34. *Trust in God*: David Fighting Goliath, I Sam. 17. Daniel in the Lion's Den, Dan. 6.

CHAPTER VI.
THE SECOND COMMANDMENT.
GOD'S NAME.

Thou shalt not take the name of the Lord thy God in vain; for the Lord will not hold him guiltless that taketh His name in vain.

What is meant by this Commandment?

We should so fear and love God as not to curse, swear, conjure, lie or deceive by His name, but call upon Him in every time of need, and worship Him with prayer, praise and thanksgiving.

THE NAME OF GOD. [Ps. 111:9, Mal. 2:2, Rev. 15:4] A name is that by which we know a person. God's name means all by which He is known to us; hence not only the words God, Lord, Jehovah, Jesus Christ, the Almighty, the Eternal, the Omniscient One, etc., but the Word of God and the Sacraments, and all holy things.

This Commandment *forbids* the wrong use, and *commands* the right use of God's holy name.

I. WHAT IS FORBIDDEN.
TAKING GOD'S NAME IN VAIN:

1. *Thoughtlessly.* God's name is taken in vain thoughtlessly by using it as an exclamation in our conversation, by reading or hearing God's Word without devotion, jesting about sacred things, quoting Scripture in fun, and the like. Thoughtlessness is no excuse. We must give an account to God for every idle word; [Matt. 12:36+] how much more for every vain use of His name.

2. *Intentionally.* This is done by those who

CURSE; [Jas. 3:9, 10, Matt. 5:44, Rom. 12:14+] that is, by those who call on God to do evil to themselves or to others. Disguised forms of cursing are sinful also.

SWEAR. We are forbidden to confirm what we say by the use of God's name, either

Needlessly [Matt. 5:34-37+] in our ordinary conversation, or

Falsely [Lev. 19:12+] before a magistrate.

There is a Legal Oath: [Deut. 6:13, Heb. 5:16] 1. Of Witness. 2. Of Innocence. 3. Of Allegiance, 4. Of Office. The oath taken by our Lord before the high-priest shows that the oath before a magistrate is not forbidden. [Matt. 26:63, 64] When taking a legal oath, we must be careful to tell the truth, the whole truth, and nothing but the truth. False swearing or perjury is a great sin. It is punished by the State, and will be punished by God. [Ezek. 17:19]

Swearing by anything besides God's name is forbidden also. [Matt. 5:34-37+]

CONJURE. [Deut. 18:10-12+] This commandment forbids all magic arts, witchcraft, sorcery, pow-wowing, fortune-telling, and all attempts by signs or formulas to discover what God has kept hidden or to attain what He has withheld. If results are obtained by such means, *e.g.*, by pow-wowing, that is no justification for their use. [Matt. 16:26] If we desire to obtain help through the use of God's name, we must pray and not conjure.

LIE. The eighth commandment forbids lying in general; this commandment forbids lying by God's name. It is broken by those who teach falsehood and error and yet declare that they are teaching God's Word. [Gal. 1:8]

DECEIVE BY HIS NAME. This is done by those who assume Christ's name by calling themselves Christians, and yet are hypocrites, and use religion as a cloak. [II Tim. 3:5+, Matt. 15:8]

Sins against this Second Commandment are common, but not small sins. God will not hold him guiltless who commits them.

II. WHAT IS COMMANDED.

We should

CALL UPON HIM. God has given us His name so that we might call upon Him for His help and grace. [Ps. 145:18+]

IN EVERY TIME OF NEED. We should call upon God in every time of trouble, danger or distress. [Ps. 50:15+] But if we call upon God only in times of special need, and do not call upon His name at other times also, we are not keeping this commandment.

AND WORSHIP HIM [Col. 3:16] in our hearts, in our homes and in church,

WITH PRAYER [Matt. 7:7+] for ourselves and for others, [I Tim. 2:1, 2]

PRAISE [Ps. 145:1] for His majesty and glory and wonderful works,
AND THANKSGIVING for temporal and spiritual blessings. [Ps. 106:1+]

QUESTIONS.—1. What is meant by God's name? 2. What does this second commandment forbid and command? 3. How is God's name taken in vain thoughtlessly? 4. How is God's name taken in vain intentionally? 5. Define cursing? 6. Define swearing? 7. What kind of swearing is forbidden? 8. What kind of swearing is permitted? 9. When taking a legal oath, what must we be careful to do? 10. Define conjuring, lying, and deceiving by God's name? 11. What is the right use of God's name? 12. Why should we call upon God? 13. When should we call upon Him? 14. Where shall we worship Him? 15. How shall we worship Him?

SCRIPTURE VERSES.—Matt. 12:36. But I say unto you, That every idle word that men shall speak, they shall give account thereof in the day of judgment.

Rom. 12:14. Bless them which persecute you: bless, and curse not.

Matt. 5:34-37. But I say unto you, Swear not at all; neither by heaven; for it is God's throne: nor by the earth; for it is his footstool: neither by Jerusalem; for it is the city of the great King. Neither shalt thou swear by thy head, because thou canst not make one hair white or black. But let your communication be Yea, yea; Nay, nay; for whatsoever is more than these cometh of evil.

Lev. 19:12. Ye shall not swear by my name falsely, neither shalt thou profane the name of thy God: I am the Lord.

Deut. 18:10-12. There shall not be found among you any one that maketh his son or his daughter to pass through the fire, or that useth divination, or an observer of times, or an enchanter, or a witch, or a charmer, or a consulter with familiar spirits, or a wizard, or a necromancer. For all that do these things are an abomination unto the LORD: and because of these abominations the LORD thy God doth drive them out from before thee.

II Tim. 3:5. Having a form of godliness, but denying the power thereof: from such turn away.

Matt. 15:8. This people draweth nigh unto me with their mouth, and honoureth me with their lips: but their heart is far from me.

Ps. 143:18. The LORD is nigh unto all them that call upon him, to all that call upon him in truth.

Ps. 50:15. Call upon me in the day of trouble: I will deliver thee, and then shalt glorify me.

Matt. 7:7. Ask, and it shall be given you; seek, and ye shall find; knock, and it shall be opened unto you.

Ps. 106:1. Praise ye the LORD. O give thanks unto the LORD; for he is good: for his mercy endureth forever.

READING.—Balaam, Numb. 22; Herod's Oath, Matt. 14:1-12; Saul and the Witch at Endor, I Sam. 28.

ILLUSTRATIONS.—*Cursing*: Job 3:1-7. Shimei, II Sam. 16:5-14. *Swearing*: Herod; Peter, Matt. 26:89-75.*Conjuring*: Saul at Endor; Bar-jesus, Acts 13:1-12. *Lying and Deceiving*: The Pharisees, Matt. 23:13-38. *Calling on God's Name*: Jesus, Matt. 26:39-44; John 17: Jacob, Gen. 32:9-12; The First Christians, Acts 2:42.

CHAPTER VII.
THE THIRD COMMANDMENT.
GOD'S DAY.

Remember the Sabbath day to keep it holy.
What is meant by this Commandment?

We should so fear and love God as not to despise His Word and the preaching of the Gospel, but deem it holy and willingly hear and learn it.

THE LORD'S DAY. Under the Old Testament the Israelites, by God's command, observed the seventh day of the week, Saturday, as the Sabbath or day of rest, because God rested from the work of Creation on the seventh day. [Gen. 2:2-3] For the Christians all days are holy. [Rom. 14:5, 6, Col. 2:16, Acts 2:46] But from the earliest times the Christian Church set apart Sunday as a special day of worship, [Acts 20:7, 1 Cor. 16:2] because it is the day on which Christ rose from the dead. The Sabbath of the Old Testament commemorated the completion of *Creation*; the Lord's Day of the New Testament commemorates the completion of *Redemption*.

A HOLY DAY. The Lord's Day is to be kept *holy* by devoting it to holy things. It is to be a day of rest in order that it may be a day of worship. Any unnecessary work or any recreation which hinders us from hearing and profiting by God's Word is sinful.

I. WHAT IS FORBIDDEN.

We are not

TO DESPISE GOD'S WORD AND THE PREACHING OF THE GOSPEL, [Luke 10:16+] by

1. Making light of God's Word, or regarding and treating it as the word of man.

2. Neglecting to go to church, and pleading poor excuses for absence. [Heb. 10:25+]

3. Inattention and lack of devotion in church. [Eccl. 5:1+]

4. Filling the mind with worldly things on Sunday (business, pleasure, Sunday-newspapers, etc.), so that God's Word cannot be rightly received into the heart. [Luke 8:5,12]

5. Making Sunday a holiday, lounging-day, or pleasure-day.

6. Making it a working-day, and thus preventing attendance at church.

II. WHAT IS COMMANDED.

We are

TO DEEM GOD'S WORD HOLY, AND WILLINGLY HEAR AND LEARN IT, by

1. Regarding it as God's voice speaking to us. [I Thess. 2:13+]

2. Going to church gladly and regularly. [Ps. 122:1, 2+]

3. Listening attentively and devoutly to God's Word, and joining heartily in the service. [Luke 11:28+, Col. 3:16, Jas. 1:21,22+, Rom. 10:17]

4. Attending Sunday-school and learning our lessons.

5. Teaching in Sunday-school when we have become old enough and our services are needed.

6. Reading the Bible and good books.

7. Doing whatever promotes the worship and honoring of God by ourselves or by others. [Jas. 1:27+]

A DAY OF REST. Sunday is meant for the good of the soul. But a rest on one day out of seven is necessary also for the welfare of the body. Sunday is a blessed privilege for body, mind, and soul. Sometimes, however, both the rest for body and mind and the attendance at church must be sacrificed in order to perform works of mercy as a duty to our fellow-men.

THE CHURCH-YEAR. The Church has also arranged a Church-year for the commemoration of the principal events in the Savior's life. The order of the Church-year is as follows: Four Sundays in Advent, Christmas, New Year, Epiphany (January 6), from two to six Sundays after Epiphany (according as Easter comes early or late); three Sundays called Septuagesima, Sexagesima, Quinquagesima; Ash Wednesday (the first day in Lent), six Sundays in Lent (the sixth being Palm Sunday), Holy Week (including Good Friday), Easter, five Sundays after Easter, Ascension Day, Sunday after Ascension, Pentecost or Whitsunday, Trinity Sunday; and from twenty-three to twenty-seven

Sundays after Trinity. The Lutheran Church observes also the festival of the Reformation on the 31st day of October. Each Sunday and Festival Day has its own Gospel and Epistle lesson, as well as its own Introit and Collect.

QUESTIONS.—1. What is the difference between Sabbath and Sunday? 2. Why is Sunday to be a day of rest? 3. What does this commandment forbid? 4. In what way is this commandment broken? 5, What does this commandment command? 6. How is this commandment to be kept? 7. Why is Sunday a blessed privilege? 8. When must our Sunday's rest and our attendance at church be sacrificed? 9. What is the object of the Church-year? 10. Give the order of the Church-year.

SCRIPTURE VERSES.—Luke 10:16. He that heareth you heareth me; and he that despiseth you despiseth me; and he that despiseth me despiseth him that sent me.

Heb. 10:25. Not forsaking the assembling of ourselves together, as the manner of some is; but exhorting one another: and so much the more, as ye see the day approaching.

Eccl. 5:1. Keep thy foot when thou goest to the house of God, and be more ready to hear, than to give the sacrifice of fools: for they consider not that they do evil.

I Thess. 2:13. When ye received the word of God which ye heard of us, ye received it not as the word of men, but, as it is in truth, the word of God, which effectually worketh also in you that believe.

Ps. 122:1, 2. I was glad when they said unto me, Let us go into the house of the LORD.

Luke 11:28. But he said, Yea, rather, blessed are they that hear the word of God, and keep it.

Jas. 1:21, 22. Receive with meekness the engrafted word, which is able to save your souls. But be ye doers of the word, and not hearers only, deceiving your own selves.

Jas. 1:27. Pure religion and undefiled before God and the Father is this, To visit the fatherless and widows in their affliction, and to keep himself unspotted from the world.

READING.—Jesus in Nazareth on the Sabbath, Luke 4:16-30.

ILLUSTRATIONS.—The Child Jesus in the Temple, Luke 2:42-52. Simeon and Anna, Luke 2:27 *seq.* Mary, Luke 10:39. The Ethiopian Eunuch, Acts 8:27 *seq.* Lydia, Acts 16:14.

THE SECOND TABLE OF THE LAW.
OUR DUTY TO OUR FELLOW-MEN.

"Thou shalt love thy neighbor as thyself." [Matt. 22:39]

OUR NEIGHBOR means every one. We are to love all men as we love ourselves; [Matt. 7:12] not only our relatives, friends, and acquaintances, but strangers, enemies, and people of all nations and climes. We must be ready to do good to all who are in need of our help and kindness. Compare the Parable of the Good Samaritan. [Luke 10:30-37]

CHAPTER VIII.
THE FOURTH COMMANDMENT.
OUR PARENTS AND SUPERIORS.

Honor thy father and thy mother, that thy days may be long upon the land which the Lord thy God giveth thee.

EXPLANATION.

What is meant by this Commandment?

We should so fear and love God as not to despise nor displease our parents and superiors, but honor, serve, obey, love and esteem them.

PARENTS are God's representatives in the family for the maintenance of law and order in it. They are charged by God with the care and training of their children, and are clothed by Him with authority over them. Their will is law for their children, so long as it does not conflict with the law of God.

SUPERIORS are those who are placed over us in a position of authority in the Family, Church, School, or State; e. g., guardians, step-parents, grand-parents, pastors, teachers, rulers, etc. They also are God's representatives to maintain order, and are to be honored and obeyed as such. In every case of a conflict of authority, we must "obey God rather than men." [Acts 5:29]

This commandment *forbids* us to despise or displease our parents and superiors, and *commands* us to honor, serve, obey, love, and esteem them.

OUR DUTY TO OUR PARENTS, GRANDPARENTS, GUARDIANS, ETC.
I. WHAT IS FORBIDDEN.

We must not

DESPISE them, mock at them, [Prov. 39:17+] make light of them, think ourselves wiser or above their authority, nor speak disrespectfully of them or to them. [Deut 27:16+]

We must not

DISPLEASE them by lack of affection, grumbling, disobedience, stubbornness, rebelliousness, or wickedness. [Exod. 21:15+]

II. WHAT IS COMMANDED.

We should

HONOR them as those who are placed over us by God's appointment, look up to them, and always treat them with proper respect [Lev. 19:3, Eph 6:2, 3+] and consideration.

SERVE them, be helpful to them, lighten their burdens, and anticipate their wishes. [I Tim. 5:4]

OBEY them by cheerfully and promptly doing their will, even when it is not to our liking. [Eph. 6:1, Col. 3:20+, Prov. 1:8]

LOVE them, and show our love by a constant desire and effort to please them. We should call to mind what they have done and still do for us, that our love for them may grow deep and tender. [John 19:26, 27]

ESTEEM them. We should regard and appreciate them as a precious gift of God. Children who have lost father or mother have met with a great loss.

IN LATER YEARS. We should honor, love and *obey* our parents while we are young; and we should still *love* and *honor* them when we are older. We must not despise or be ashamed of them if we happen to rise to a higher position in life than they. When they have grown old and feeble, we should care tenderly for them; and after they are dead, we should treasure their memory.

OUR DUTY TO OUR SUPERIORS. [Rom. 13:7+]

The Pastor is to be honored for the sake of the office which he holds. He is the ambassador of Christ; [II Cor. 5:20] and when he preaches the Gospel, or speaks words of admonition and counsel in private, the Saviour speaks through him. Those who hear him hear Christ; those who despise him despise Christ. [Luke 10:16] We should heed his admonitions, [Heb. 13:17+, I Thess. 5:12, 13] and, as far as we are able, help and encourage him in his work.

Our Teachers in Sunday-school and in other schools are placed over us in a position of authority, and must therefore be respected and honored.

Rulers and the Government. The State is God's servant to regulate temporal affairs and to maintain law and order in the land. Rulers and officials of the government must be respected and honored. [Matt. 22:21+, Rom. 13:1-4+] Christians must be good citizens.

They must always obey the law, so long as it does not conflict with the law of God. [I Pet. 2:13, Acts 5:29] They should be patriotic, pray for their country, be ready to defend it, pay their taxes, and be concerned that it shall be a Christian land. Every voter shares in the responsibility of securing righteous government, and should cast his vote conscientiously.

OLD PERSONS in general are to be treated with respect and honor. [Lev. 19:32+]

A special blessing is promised to those who keep this commandment.

QUESTIONS.—1. What does the Second Table of the Law teach? 2. What is meant by "our neighbor"? 3. What is the position of parents in the family? 4. What is meant by "superiors"? 5. To whom is our highest obedience due? 6. What does this commandment forbid, and what does it command? 7. In order to avoid despising or displeasing our parents, what should we not do? 8. Why and how should we honor them? 9. How should we serve them? 10. How should we obey them? 11. How should we show our love to them? 12. What should we always remember concerning our parents? 13. What is meant by esteeming them? 14. How should we regard and treat them when we have grown older? 15. What is our duty to our pastor? 16. What is our duty to our teachers? 17. Why should we honor our rulers? 18. What are a Christian's duties to his country? 19. How must we treat old persons in general? 20. What special blessing is promised to those who keep this commandment?

SCRIPTURE VERSES.—Prov. 30:17. The eye that mocketh at his father, and despiseth to obey his mother, the ravens of the valley shall pick it out, and the young eagles shall eat it.

Deut. 27:16. Cursed be he that setteth light by his father or his mother: and all the people shall say, Amen.

Exod. 21:15. And he that smiteth his father, or his mother, shall be surely put to death.

Eph. 6:2, 3. Honour thy father and mother; which is the first commandment with promise; that it may be well with thee, and thou mayest live long on the earth.

Col. 3:20. Children, obey your parents in all things: for this is well pleasing unto the Lord.

Rom. 13:7. Render therefore to all their dues: tribute to whom tribute is due; custom to whom custom; fear to whom fear; honour to whom honour.

Heb. 13:17. Obey them that have the rule over you, and submit yourselves: for they watch for your souls, as they that must give account, that they may do it with joy, and not with grief: for that is unprofitable for you.

Matt. 22:21. Render therefore unto Caesar the things which are Caesar's; and unto God the things that are God's.

Rom. 13:1. Let every soul be subject unto the higher powers. For there is no power but of God: the powers that be are ordained of God.

Lev. 19:32. Thou shall rise up before the hoary head, and honor the face of the old man, and fear thy God: I am the LORD.

READING.—Joseph and his Father, Gen. 47:1-12.

ILLUSTRATIONS.—*Despising and displeasing parents*: Jacob's sons, Gen. 37; Eli's sons, I Sam. 2:22-25; Absalom, II Sam. 25. *Honoring them*: Jesus, Luke 2:51.

CHAPTER IX.
THE FIFTH COMMANDMENT.
HUMAN LIFE.

Thou shall not kill.

What is meant by this Commandment?

We should so fear and love God as not to do our neighbor any bodily harm or injury, but rather assist and comfort him in danger and want.

Human life is sacred. It is man's most precious earthly possession; for without it he cannot enjoy any other. This commandment is meant to guard it. We dare not shorten another person's life, nor our own. God gives life, and He alone has the right to take it away.

This commandment *forbids* us to kill or injure other persons or ourselves. It *commands* us to assist and comfort our neighbor in danger and want.

I. WHAT is FORBIDDEN.

We must not

1. KILL OR INJURE OTHER PERSONS.

Murder. To destroy any human life, even if it be very young or yet unborn, is a great crime. He who commits murder is to be punished with death. [Gen. 9:6+] Among the motives which prompt to murder are anger, hatred, [Gen. 4:1-8] envy, [Gen. 37] jealousy, revenge, [Matt. 14:3-11, Rom. 12:19+] frivolity, avarice, robbery, and a desire to hide past sin. [II Sam. 11] We must be on our guard against all that would ever tempt us to this great crime.

Duels. It is foolish as well as sinful to pretend to establish the right or wrong of a question by a duel.

Unjust Wars are wholesale murder. Rulers must do all that they honorably can to prevent war. Yet as a last resort to maintain the right, war is justifiable.

Hatred is murder in the heart. "He that hateth his brother is a murderer." [I John 3:15, Matt. 5:21, 22+, Eph. 4:31, 32+]

Tempting Others to useless risks in which they may perish or be injured, or to drunkenness, dissipation, etc. which will shorten their life, is a transgression of this commandment.

Causing Accidents by neglect, carelessness or bad workmanship, or

Shortening Other People's Lives [Gen. 37:31-35] by maltreatment, overwork, worriment, etc. makes men guilty of sin against this commandment.

Neglect to Warn others of impending danger *or neglect to assist* them in need may result in their injury or death.

The law recognizes our right to defend our life when it is unjustly assailed. But killing others in self-defense must he our last resort. Many persons act hastily. The official who inflicts the death penalty on condemned criminals is not guilty of wrong, but is doing his duty as an officer of the State. [Rom 13:4]

It is a sin to kill our neighbor's *soul* by tempting him to sin, or enticing him to wrong-doing by our evil example.

We must not

2.—KILL OR INJURE OURSELVES.

Suicide is often prompted by despair, remorse, [Matt. 27:35] cowardice, recklessness, or insanity. But it is sinful as well as foolish and cowardly. He who commits it robs himself of the opportunity to repent, and leaves others to bear the burdens from which he shrank. If we are tempted to despair, we should not commit suicide, but seek comfort and strength in God's Word. If we have fallen into disgrace by sin, we should repent and lead a better life.

Duels. We not only have no right to endanger another's life by a duel, but we have no right to endanger our own. The duel, which was once a common practice, has justly fallen under the condemnation of public opinion.

A Life of Sin. Impurity, drunkenness, gluttony, or dissipation will shorten our life, and make us die before our allotted time.

Disregard of the Laws of Health, overwork, needless exposure, carelessness, violent anger, needless worry, are all forbidden by this commandment.

The voluntary sacrifice of our life for truth and right (martyrdom), or in defense of our country, or in an effort to rescue and save others, is not only justifiable but noble. [I John 3:16]

II. WHAT IS COMMANDED.

We should ASSIST AND COMFORT OUR NEIGHBOR. [Gal. 6:10+, Luke 10:30-35, Matt. 5:7+, Matt. 5:44+, Rom. 12:20, Matt. 22:39, Matt. 7:12+, Prov. 24:17]

1. IN DANGER. We should Warn him of danger. Defend and rescue him. Ward off danger from him. Save him from worry and anxiety whenever we can.

2. IN WANT. We should Aid the poor and destitute. Minister to the sick. Comfort the afflicted and distressed. Give to organized charities: orphanages, asylums, hospitals, rescue-work, etc. Give to missions in order to save souls.

QUESTIONS.—1. What is to be said about the sacredness of human life? 2. What does this fifth commandment forbid? 3. What does it command? 4. Whom are we forbidden to kill or injure? 5. Mention some ways in which this commandment is broken with respect to others. 6. What is to be said about the sin of murder and its punishment? 7. What are some of the motives which prompt men to murder? 8. What is to be said about duels? 9. Is war right? 10. What does the Bible say about hatred? 11. What is to be said about useless risks, accidents, maltreatment, etc.? 12. What is to be said about neglecting to warn or assist others? 13. What is to be said about the right of self-defense? 14. What is to be said about the official who inflicts the death-penalty on criminals? 15. Mention some ways in which this commandment is broken with respect to self. 16. What motives prompt men to suicide, and how should we guard against such a sin? 17. What is to be said about the folly and cowardice of the suicide's act? 18. What is to be said of the voluntary sacrifice of our life? 19. How are we to assist our neighbor in danger? 20. How are we to assist and comfort him in want?

SCRIPTURE VERSES.—Gen. 9:6. Whoso sheddeth man's blood, by man shall his blood be shed; for in the image of God made he man.

Rom. 12:19. Dearly beloved, avenge not yourselves, but rather give place unto wrath; for it is written, Vengeance is mine; I will repay, saith the Lord.

Matt. 5:21, 22. Ye have heard that it was said by them of old time, Thou shalt not kill; and whosoever shall kill shall be in danger of the judgment: but I say unto you, That whosoever is angry with his brother without a cause shall be in danger of the judgment; and whosoever shall say to his brother, Raca, shall be in danger of the council; but whosoever shall say, Thou fool, shall be in danger of hell fire.

Eph. 4:31, 32. Let all bitterness, and wrath, and anger, and clamour, and evil speaking, be put away from you, with all malice; and be ye kind one to another, tender-hearted, forgiving one another, even as God for Christ's sake hath forgiven you.

Gal. 6:10. As we have therefore opportunity, let us do good unto all men, especially unto them who are of the household of faith.

Matt, 5:7. Blessed are the merciful: for they shall obtain mercy.

Matt. 5:44, 45. But I say unto you, Love your enemies, bless them that curse you, do good to them that hate you, and pray for them which despitefully use you, and persecute you: that ye may be the children of your Father which is in heaven.

Matt. 7:12. Therefore all things whatsoever ye would that men should do to you, do ye even so to them: for this is the law and the prophets.

READING.—Cain kills Abel. Gen. 4:1-16.

ILLUSTRATIONS.—*Murder*: Cain; Joab, II Sam. 3:22, 29; Ahab and Jezebel, I Kings 21:1-19; Herod, Matt. 2:16-18. *Hatred*: Joseph's Brethren, Gen. 37. *Suicide*: Saul, I Sam. 31:5; Judas, Matt. 27:5. *Assisting and Comforting*: The Good Samaritan, Luke, 10:25-37.

CHAPTER X.
THE SIXTH COMMANDMENT.
PURITY. MARRIAGE.

Thou shalt not commit adultery.

What is meant by this Commandment?

We should so fear and love God as to be chaste and pure in our words and deeds, each one also loving and honoring his wife or her husband.

This commandment is meant to preserve our personal purity, and to guard the holy estate of marriage. It *forbids* adultery and all impurity. It *commands* chastity and purity in thought, word, and deed.

I. PURITY.

We should be CHASTE AND PURE

In Heart. We should keep our heart free from impure thoughts and desires. [Matt. 5:8+, Prov. 4:23+, Ps. 51:10] God judges us by the state of our heart. [I Sam. 16:7] Unchaste thoughts must not be delighted in nor harbored, but subdued and stamped out. They poison the soul. They are themselves a transgression of this commandment, [Matt. 5:28+] and they lead to further transgressions of it by word and deed.

IN WORDS. We must avoid immodest conversation, unchaste words, vile stories, and shameless jests. [Eph. 5:3-4, Eph. 4:29+] Such things are not smart, as many think, but vile and despicable. We should never take part in nor listen to a conversation which we would be ashamed to have overheard by persons whom we respect.

IN DEEDS. We should carefully avoid every act which would bring the blush of shame to our cheeks if it were known to our parents or others whose opinion we cherish. Our bodies are to be God's temple, [I Cor. 6:19, 20+] and they dare not be given over to sin and impurity. [Rom. 6:13] We should remember that God sees even in secret, and knows all our actions. [Ps. 139:1-12]

Impurity of heart and life will not go unpunished. [I Cor. 3:16, 17+, Gal. 5:19-21+] It is often followed by the most dreadful consequences: a ruined body, an enfeebled mind, a poisoned soul, a tortured conscience, public shame, dreadful disease and an untimely death.

To Keep ourselves Pure we should watch and pray, [Matt. 26:41+] avoid idleness, evil company, bad books and papers, indecent songs and pictures, immoral plays, intemperance in eating and drinking, and all that would incite to impurity. We should keep our minds occupied with good thoughts and desires, so that we have no room for evil ones. [Rom. 13:14]

II. MARRIAGE.

Marriage is the union of one man and one woman for life in the bonds of love and faithfulness.

A Holy Estate. Marriage was instituted by God in Eden [Gen. 2:13] and was sanctioned by Christ, who performed His first miracle at a wedding. [John 2:1-11] It is a holy estate. Celibacy is not a holier estate than marriage, as the Roman Catholic Church maintains. [I Tim. 4:1-3]

Indissoluble. The marriage tie is binding until one of the married persons dies. [Matt. 19:6+] Except by death, the marriage relation cannot be broken or dissolved without sin against this sixth commandment. [Matt. 5:32+, Matt 19:9] If one party to the marriage is guilty of adultery, the innocent party may obtain a divorce. No other divorces are allowed by Christ.

An Important Step. Marriage is a most important step in life. It must not be entered into hastily or thoughtlessly. If a mistake is made in the choice of a partner for life, the mistake can never be remedied. Those who contemplate such a step should pray for God's guidance. Marriage should not be entered upon for money, social advantages, and the like, but for love. Parents should be consulted. While marriage by a civil magistrate is valid, Christians should seek God's blessing upon their union and be married by His ordained servant. The laws of the State must be carefully obeyed. Marriage between near relatives is forbidden by God's Word. [Lev. 18] Those who are married should, if possible, be of the same faith. Marriages between Protestants and Roman Catholics are seldom happy.

Duty of Husband [Eph. 5:25+, Col. 3:19] *and Wife.* [Eph. 5:22+, Col. 3:18] EACH SHOULD LOVE AND HONOR HIS WIFE OR HER HUSBAND. The man is the head of the family, but he must not be a tyrant. The wife is not his slave, but his dearest companion. They are no longer two but one, with a common love, a common life, a common property, common children, common hopes and aspirations, and a common Saviour. [I Pet. 3:7, I Pet. 3:1] They should be patient with one another's faults, just to one another's virtues, and should unselfishly seek one another's happiness. They should live together in mutual love and faithfulness till separated by death. Only when husband and wife continue to love and honor one another can they be happy. The breaking of the marriage covenant is followed by shame and misery.

QUESTIONS.—1. What is this commandment meant to preserve and guard? 2. What does it forbid and command? 3. What is it to be said about purity of heart? 4. What is to be said about purity in words? 5. What is to be said about purity in deeds? 6. Mention some of the consequences which often follow upon impurity. 7. How may we keep ourselves pure? 8. What is marriage? 9. Why is marriage a holy estate? 10. How long is the marriage tie binding? 11. When only and by whom dare a divorce be obtained? 12. Why must marriage not be entered upon hastily or thoughtlessly? 13. What care should be exercised by those who think of being married? 14. What is the duty of husband and wife?

SCRIPTURE VERSES.—Matt. 5:8. Blessed are the pure in heart: for they shall see God.

Prov. 4:23. Keep thy heart with all diligence; for out of it are the issues of life.

Matt. 5:28. But I say unto you, That whosoever looketh on a woman to lust after her hath committed adultery with her already in his heart.

Eph. 4:29. Let no corrupt communication proceed out of your mouth, but that which is good to the use of edifying, that it may minister grace unto the hearers.

I Cor. 6:19, 20. What I know ye not that your body is the temple of the Holy Ghost which is in you, which ye have of God, and ye are not your own? For ye are bought with a price; therefore glorify God in your body and in your spirit, which are God's.

I Cor. 3:16, 17. Know ye not that ye are the temple of God, and that the Spirit of God dwelleth in you? If any man defile the temple of God, him shall God destroy: for the temple of God is holy; which temple ye are.

Gal. 5:19-21. Now the works of the flesh are manifest, which are these, adultery, fornication, uncleanness, lasciviousness, idolatry, witchcraft, hatred, variance, emulations, wrath, strife, seditions, heresies, envyings, murders, drunkenness, revellings, and such like: of the which I tell you before, as I have also told you in time past, that they which, do such things shall not inherit the kingdom of God.

Matt. 26:41, Watch and pray, that ye enter not into temptation: the spirit indeed is willing, but the flesh is weak.

Matt. 19: 6. What therefore God hath joined together, let not man put asunder.

Matt. 5:32. But I say unto you, That whosoever shall put away his wife, saving for the cause of fornication, causeth her to commit adultery: and whosoever shall marry her that is divorced committeth adultery.

Eph. 5:25, Husbands, love your wives, even as Christ also loved the church, and gave himself for it.

Eph. 5:22. Wives, submit yourselves unto your own husbands, as unto the Lord.

READING.—The Creation of Eve, Gen. 2:18-25; or, The Marriage at Cana, John 2:1-11.

CHAPTER XI.
THE SEVENTH COMMANDMENT.
PROPERTY. HONESTY.

Thou shalt not steal.
What is meant by this commandment?
We should so fear and love God as not to rob our neighbor of his money or property, nor bring it into our possession by unfair dealing or fraudulent means, but rather assist him to improve and protect it.

The object of this commandment is to protect every man in the possession of that which is lawfully his own. Without such protection the individual could not support his life, and society could not exist. The industrious and thrifty would be at the mercy of the lazy and wicked. This commandment *forbids* us to use dishonest means of acquiring property. It *commands* us to assist our neighbor to improve and protect his own.

PROPERTY consists of whatever each person lawfully acquires of the earth's lands, forests, water, mines, houses, goods or money. It may be rightfully acquired by original claim, inheritance, gift, or labor of body or mind. Honest labor united with economy is the best way to acquire it.

UNEQUAL DIVISION. God, who is the absolute owner of all things, [I Cor. 10:26] divides to each as He will. [Jer. 27:5] He "maketh poor and maketh rich." [I Sam. 2:7, Prov. 22:2+] Much poverty, however, is due to men's own laziness, idleness, [II Thess. 3:10+] carelessness or extravagance; and much wealth has been wrongfully gained contrary to God's will as expressed in this commandment. *Communism*, or the equal division of property among all men, is not practicable. It failed in the apostolic Church. [Acts 5:1-10] If all things were equally divided, some would soon clamor for another division.

POVERTY AND RICHES. The happiest person is he who is neither rich nor poor, but has sufficient for his needs. [Prov. 30:7-9+, Prov. 15:16-17+] Poverty may tempt a man to dishonesty; and riches may lead him to avarice, hardness of heart, worldliness and extravagance. [I Tim. 6:9, 10, I Tim. 6:17+] Riches make it hard for a man to enter into the kingdom of God. [Matt. 19:24+, Matt. 13:22] We should respect men for what they are, and not for what they have. We should not flatter the rich nor despise the poor. [Jas. 2:1-4]

USE OF PROPERTY. God entrusts earthly property to us as His stewards. [Luke 19:12-27, Matt. 25:14-30, Luke 16:1-8] Whether we are rich or poor, we should so use our property as to be able to give an account to God. *For ourselves* and those dependent on us [I Tim. 5:8+] we should use it for the supply of our bodily needs (food, clothing, shelter, a reasonable amount of pleasure) and of our spiritual needs [Luke 12:15+, Matt. 6:33, I Cor. 9:14] (the Church and the Gospel). *For our fellow-men* we should, when necessary, use it according to our ability for their bodily needs (the poor) and their spiritual needs (Home and Foreign Missions). [Matt. 22:39]

I. WHAT IS FORBIDDEN.

1. ROBBING OUR NEIGHBOR. The grossest forms of dishonesty are Robbery, Theft, Burglary, Embezzlement, and Forgery. These are recognized by all as wrong. But it is also wrong to bring our neighbor's property into our possession, by

2. UNFAIR DEALING AND FRAUDULENT MEANS, [Prov. 29:24, Lev. 6:2, 3, Ps. 37:21, Jer. 22:13, Lev. 19:35, 36, Hab. 2:6, Prov. 15:6, Deut. 24:14, Jas. 5:4, Prov. 11:1] such as Concealing stolen property, Withholding lost or borrowed property, Evading taxes, Refusing to pay debts, Wilful idleness and beggary, Betting and gambling, Lotteries and chancing, Bribery, Useless lawsuits, Negligent management of another's property, Stealing car-rides, Unfaithful labor, Insufficient wages, Cornering the market,

Overcharging, Usury, Adulterating goods, Giving short weight or measure, and Cheating of any kind.

3. *Dishonesty in the Heart.* Dishonesty has its source in the covetousness and greed of the human heart. [Mic. 2:2] Men first covet, and then steal or defraud. We must beware of covetousness. [Luke 12:15+] The love of money is a root of all evil. [I Tim. 6:10+] We must be honest even in small matters. He who is dishonest in little will be dishonest in much. [Luke 16:10] We must avoid all that would tempt us to dishonesty; namely, evil companions, idleness, speculation, extravagance, etc.

II. WHAT IS COMMANDED.

We should

1. ASSIST OUR NEIGHBOR TO IMPROVE AND PROTECT HIS PROPERTY. [Exod. 23:4, 5, Matt. 7:12] We should help him to get along well in the world, and do what we can to prevent him from being deprived of his possessions.

2. *Restore to the real owner* whatever has been dishonestly gotten. [Luke 19:8]

3. *Be Ready to use our money* and property in order to help and benefit our neighbor. [Eph. 4:28+, Heb. 13.18+, I Pet. 4:10] We must be helpful and charitable toward our fellow-men.

QUESTIONS.—1. What is the object of the seventh commandment? 2. What does this commandment forbid? 3. What does it command? 4. How may property be rightfully acquired? 5. Explain why property is unequally divided among men? 6. What is to be said about communism? 7. Why is he who is neither rich nor poor the happiest man? 8. What is the right use of property? 9. Mention some gross forms of dishonesty? 10. Mention some other ways in which this commandment is broken? 11. Where does dishonesty have its source? 12. If we would be honest, what must we guard against? 13. In what ways does this commandment require us to assist our neighbor?

SCRIPTURE VERSES—Prov. 22:2. The rich and poor meet together: the LORD is the maker of them all.

II Thess. 3:10. This we commanded you, that if any would not work, neither should he eat.

Prov. 30:7-9. Two things have I required of thee; deny me them not before I die: Remove far from me vanity and lies; give me neither poverty nor riches; feed me with food convenient for me: lest I be full, and deny thee, and say, Who is the LORD? or lest I be poor, and steal, and take the name of my God in vain.

Prov. 15:16-17. Better is little with the fear of the LORD, than great treasure and trouble therewith. Better is a dinner of herbs where love is, than a stalled ox and hatred therewith.

I Tim. 6:17. Charge them that are rich in this world, that they be not highminded, nor trust in uncertain riches, but in the living God, who giveth us richly all things to enjoy.

Matt. 19:24. And again I say unto you, It is easier for a camel to go through the eye of a needle, than for a rich man to enter into the kingdom of God.

I Tim. 5:8. But if any provide not for his own, and specially for those of his own house, he hath denied the faith, and is worse than an infidel.

Luke 12:15. And he said unto them, Take heed, and beware of covetousness: for a man's life consisteth not in the abundance of the things which he possesseth.

I Tim. 6:10. For the love of money is the root of all evil: which while some coveted after, they have erred from the faith, and pierced themselves through with many sorrows.

Eph. 4:28. Let him that stole steal no more: but rather let him labour, working with his hands the thing which is good, that he may have to give to him that needeth.

Heb. 13:16. But to do good and to communicate forget not: for with such sacrifices God is well pleased.

READING.—The Unjust Steward, Luke 16:1-7; or, Matt. 25: 31-46.

ILLUSTRATIONS.—*Poverty and Riches*: The Rich Man and Lazarus, Luke 16:19-31; The Rich Fool, Luke 12:15-21; The Prodigal Son, Luke 15:11 seq. *Dishonesty*: Achan, Josh. 7. Gehazi, II Kings 5. Judas, Luke 12:6, Ananias and Sapphira, Acts 5. *Benevolence*: The Good Samaritan, Luke 10:30-37; Dorcas, Acts 9:36; Cornelius, Acts 10:2.

CHAPTER XII.
THE EIGHTH COMMANDMENT.
TRUTHFULNESS.

Thou shalt not bear false witness against thy neighbor.

What is meant by this commandment?

We should so fear and love God as not deceitfully to belie, betray, slander, nor raise injurious reports against our neighbor, but apologize for him, speak well of him, and put the most charitable construction on all his actions.

THE OBJECT of this commandment is to secure truthfulness, [Eph. 4:25+] and to guard our good name. [Prov. 22:1+] Without truthfulness we could not believe anything we heard, and the utmost confusion would prevail in the affairs of men. A good name is one of our most precious earthly possessions.

This commandment *forbids* all lying. It *commands* perfect truthfulness and a charitable judgment of others.

I. WHAT IS FORBIDDEN.

ALL LYING is forbidden. [Ps. 34:13+] False witness against other *persons* is the worst form of lying. All lesser forms of lying are forbidden along with the greater.

1. *False Witness against our Neighbor.* We must not tell a falsehood about another person either in court or in every-day life. We must not

BELIE him, that is, tell an untruth about him.

BETRAY. [Prov. 11:13+, Prov. 24:28] We must not abuse our neighbor's confidence by revealing his innocent secrets, and thus annoying or harming him. One who pretends to be another's friend, and yet betrays him, is acting a lie. We dare not, however, hide crime; and we must tell what we know about others if the court, or parents, or persons who have a right to know, inquire of us.

SLANDER NOR RAISE INJURIOUS REPORTS. [Exod. 23:1+, Lev. 19:16, Ps. 15:1-3] We must not invent nor repeat false reports concerning our neighbor. We must not say behind his back what we fear to say to his face. We must not magnify his faults, [Matt. 7:3-5] nor impute evil motives to him, nor make his words and conduct look as bad as possible. The slanderer is worse than a thief and causes incalculable suffering and misery. [Prov. 25:18+, Jas. 3:5-8] We should remember that words once spoken live on for good or evil, and cannot be unsaid; and that we must give an account to God for every word we speak. [Matt. 12:36]

2. *Lying of Any Kind.* A lie is a conscious falsehood uttered with the purpose of deceiving. It may be acted as well as spoken. [Prov. 6:13] We must not deceive nor try to deceive others by telling an untruth, by hiding the truth or a part of it, by hypocrisy, flattery, boasting, broken promises, conventional lies, "white lies," "lies of necessity," guesses given as facts, etc.

II. WHAT IS COMMANDED.

1. *Truthfulness.* Truth is of God; [Deut. 32:4] lying is of the devil. [John 8:44] As children of God we must be truthful. [Col. 3:9+] A liar is an abomination in God's sight. [Prov. 12:22, Prov. 17:15] If necessary, we should be ready to suffer and die for the truth.

2. *A Charitable Judgment of Others.* We should

APOLOGIZE FOR OUR NEIGHBOR, and defend him when his character is unjustly assailed. [Matt. 7:12, Prov. 31:8, 9] We must be careful, however, not to excuse or make light of sin. [Isa. 5:20+] We should

SPEAK WELL OF HIM whenever we can do so truthfully. We should speak of his virtues rather than of his faults. [Matt. 7:1, 2+, Jas. 4:11] If we cannot speak well of him, then, unless it is absolutely necessary, we had better not speak of him at all. We should

PUT THE MOST CHARITABLE CONSTRUCTION ON ALL HIS ACTIONS. [I Pet. 4:8+, I Cor. 13:4-7, Gal. 6:1] We should, as far as possible, make the best and not the worst of what our neighbor says and does. We should think and speak of him only in kindness.

QUESTIONS.—1. What a the object of this commandment? 2. What does it forbid? 3. What does it command? 4. What is the worst form of lying? 5. What is included under false witness? 6. What is meant by belying our neighbor? 7. What is to be said about betraying him? 8. What is to be said about slander and the slanderer? 9. Define a lie. 10. In what ways do men speak and act lies? 11. Why should we be truthful? 12. What is to be said about apologizing for our neighbor? 13. What rule should we follow in speaking of others? 14. How should we think and speak of our neighbor?

SCRIPTURE VERSES.—Eph. 4:25. Wherefore putting away lying, speak every man truth with his neighbour: for we are members one of another.

Prov. 22:1. A good name is rather to be chosen than great riches, and loving favour rather than silver and gold.

Ps. 34:13. Keep thy tongue from evil, and thy lips from speaking guile.

Prov. 11:13. A talebearer revealeth secrets: but he that is of a faithful spirit concealeth the matter.

Exod. 23:1. Thou shalt not raise a false report: put not thine hand with the wicked to be an unrighteous witness.

Matt. 7:3-5. And why beholdest thou the mote that is in thy brother's eye, but considerest not the beam that is in thine own eye? Or how wilt thou say to thy brother, Let me pull out the mote out of thine eye; and, behold, a beam is in thine own eye? Thou hypocrite, first cast out the beam out of thine own eye; and then shalt thou see clearly to cast out the mote out of thy brother's eye.

Prov. 25:18. A man that beareth false witness against his neighbour is a maul, and a sword, and a sharp arrow.

Col. 3:9. Lie not one to another, seeing that ye have put off the old man with his deeds.

Is. 5:20. Woe unto them that call evil good, and good evil; that put darkness for light, and light for darkness; that put bitter for sweet, and sweet for bitter!

Matt. 7:1, 2. Judge not, that ye be not judged. For with what judgment ye judge, ye shall be judged: and with what measure ye mete, it shall be measured to you again.

I Pet. 4:8. And above all things have fervent charity among yourselves: for charity shall cover the multitude of sins.

READING.—The False Witnesses against Stephen, Acts 6:8-15.

ILLUSTRATIONS.—*False Witness*: Against Christ, Matt. 26:60; against Naboth, I Kings 21:10; against Paul, Acts 25:7. *Slander*: Absalom against David, II Sam. 15:1 seq.; *Lying*: Jacob, Gen. 27:19; Jacob's Sons, Gen. 37:32. *Betrayal*: Judas. *Speaking well*: Jonathan, I Sam. 19:4.

CHAPTER XIII.
THE NINTH AND TENTH COMMANDMENTS.
A RIGHT HEART.

Thou shalt not covet thy neighbor's house.
What is meant by this Commandment?
We should so fear and love God as not to desire by craftiness to gain possession of our neighbor's inheritance or home, or to obtain it under the pretext of a legal right; but be ready to assist and serve him in the preservation of his own.

Thou shalt not covet thy neighbor's wife, nor his manservant, nor his maid-servant, nor his ox, nor his ass, nor anything that is thy neighbor's.
What is meant by this Commandment?
We should so fear and love God as not to alienate our neighbor's wife from him, entice away his servants, nor let loose his cattle, but use our endeavors that they may remain and discharge their duty to him.

Both these commandments forbid coveting; hence, we may consider them together. They deal with the root and source of all sin; namely, the evil lusts and desires of the heart. [Matt. 15:19+, Jas. 1:14, 15]

THE OBJECT of these two commandments is to emphasize the necessity of a right state of heart. [I Sam. 16:7+, Matt. 5:5] All the commandments must, indeed, be kept in thought as well as in word and deed. But by adding these two special commandments against coveting, God desires to impress upon us most strongly that wrong thoughts and desires make us guilty before Him. We are not keeping God's commandments unless we are free from the *desire* to transgress them. As a man "thinketh in his heart, so is he." [Prov. 23:7]

THE HEART BY NATURE SINFUL. We are born with a sinful nature and a natural inclination to evil (Original sin), which we have inherited from our ancestors as a result of the fall into sin. [John 3:6+, Jer. 17:9] This natural inclination to evil manifests itself in wrong thoughts and desires which arise in the heart. [Rom. 7:18, 19+] These wrong desires or lusts are in themselves sinful: and if they are not subdued, they lead to sins of words and deeds. [Jas. 1:14, 15+]

These commandments *forbid* us to covet anything that is our neighbor's. They *command* us to assist and serve him in retaining his own.

I. WHAT IS FORBIDDEN.

COVETING, To covet means to desire what we have no right to have. To wish to obtain something in a lawful way is not coveting. But we must not have

1. *An Unlawful Desire* [Gal. 5:24+] for our neighbor's possessions, whether it be his property, wife, servants, cattle, or anything that is his. We must not envy him on account of them, nor begrudge them to him, nor wish that we had them in his stead. We must not make

2. *Any Attempt to Gratify such Unlawful Desires* and TO GAIN POSSESSION OF OUR NEIGHBOR'S INHERITANCE OR HOME

BY CRAFTINESS, shrewdness, cunning, deceit and the like. [Prov. 15:6] Nor dare we seek TO OBTAIN IT

UNDER THE PRETEXT OF A LEGAL RIGHT; that is, by ways which human laws allow and appear to sanction, but which are not right before God. [Matt. 23:14+] Nor dare we attempt to

ALIENATE (estrange), ENTICE or drive away from him his wife, servants, or cattle, by persuasion, flattery, falsehood, promises, threats, or force.

II. WHAT is COMMANDED.

ASSISTANCE AND SERVICE. We should

1. ASSIST AND SERVE HIM IN THE PRESERVATION OF HIS OWN. [Phil. 2:4+, Gal. 5:12] Instead of wishing to get his property away from him, we should most heartily wish that he may be able to keep it, and should help him to retain it. We should

2. USE OUR ENDEAVORS THAT THEY who belong to him MAY REMAIN AND DISCHARGE THEIR DUTY TO HIM. We should help him to retain their

affection and faithfulness. We should heartily wish them to remain, and persuade them to do so.

QUESTIONS.—1. Why may these two commandments be considered together? 2. With what do they deal? 3. What is the object of these two commandments? 4. When only are we keeping God's commandments? 5. What is to be said about the natural state of the heart. 6. What do these commandments forbid? 7. What do they command? 8. Define coveting. 9. If we would avoid breaking this commandment, what must we not do? 10. How should we be of assistance and service to our neighbor?

SCRIPTURE VERSES.—Matt. 15:19. For out of the heart proceed evil thoughts, murders, adulteries, fornications, thefts, false witness, blasphemies.

I Sam. 16:7. The LORD seeth not as man seeth; for man looketh on the outward appearance, but the LORD looketh on the heart.

John 3:6. That which is born of the flesh, is flesh; and that which is born of the Spirit is spirit.

Rom. 7:18, 19. For I know that in me (that is, in my flesh) dwelleth no good thing: for to will is present with me; but how to perform that which is good I find not. For the good that I would, I do not: but the evil which I would not, that I do.

Jas. 1:14, 15. But every man is tempted, when he is drawn away of his own lust, and enticed. Then when lust hath conceived, it bringeth forth sin; and sin, when it is finished, bringeth forth death.

Gal. 5:24. And they that are Christ's have crucified the flesh with the affections and lusts.

Matt. 23:14. Woe unto you, scribes and Pharisees, hypocrites! for ye devour widows' houses, and for a pretence make long prayer: therefore, ye shall receive the greater damnation.

Phil. 2:4. Look not every man on his own things, but every man also on the things of others.

READING.—Naboth's Vineyard, I Kings 21:1-19.

ILLUSTRATIONS.—*Coveting*: Ahab; David, II Sam. 12; Absalom, II Sam. 15. *Assistance and Service*: Paul, Philemon 10-17.

CHAPTER XIV.
THE CONCLUSION OF THE COMMANDMENTS.
PUNISHMENT OR BLESSING.

What does God declare concerning these Commandments?

He says: "I the Lord thy God am a jealous God, visiting the iniquity of the fathers upon the children unto the third and fourth generation of them that hate me, and showing mercy unto thousands of them that love me and keep my commandments,"

What in meant by this Declaration?

God threatens to punish all those who transgress these commandments; we should therefore dread His displeasure and not act contrarily to these commandments. But He promises grace and every blessing to all who keep them; we should therefore love and trust in him, and cheerfully do what he has commanded us.

A JEALOUS GOD. God claims our highest love, and is grieved and offended if we turn our affections away from Him and disobey His law. He will punish or bless men according as they hate or love Him: [Rom. 2:6-10, Deut. 11:26-28, Gal. 6:7-8] "to the third and fourth generation of them that hate him," and "unto thousands of them that love Him and keep His commandments."

I. PUNISHMENT.

GOD THREATENS TO PUNISH

1. *Whom?* ALL THOSE WHO TRANSGRESS THESE COMMANDMENTS [Rom: 1:18+, Lev 26:14-15, Isa 59:2, Ezek. 18:4+, Rom. 6:23+] by commission, (doing what is forbidden) or omission (not doing what is commanded), whether it be transgression by deed or word or thought. Every transgression, great or small, is sin, and makes men guilty and punishable. [Gal. 3:10]

2. *Why?* Because justice demands it. [Gal. 6:7+] God cannot be unjust. He cannot overlook or excuse sin. [Eccl. 11:9] Earthly governments must and do punish offenders, or they would be unjust to those persons who obey the law. A law without a penalty would amount to nothing. God, who governs the universe, is and must be just. [Gen. 18:25+]

3. *How?*

In this World God punishes sin by Pangs of Conscience; [Matt. 26:75, Matt. 27:3-4] Pains and Sufferings which are the results of wrong-doing, [Jer. 17:10] *e.g.*, the results of drunkenness and licentiousness; Legal Penalties which the State, as God's servant to punish crime, inflicts by fines, imprisonment and hanging; [Rom. 13:4] Special Judgments upon individuals [1 Cor. 10:5] in the form of sickness, accidents and reverses, though we must remember that afflictions are not always a judgment, but are often sent upon the godly as a chastening; [Heb. 12:6+] General Judgments upon wicked communities, such as that which God sent upon Sodom and Gomorrah. [Gen. 19:24]

Children are often obliged to suffer for the sins of their parents. [Jer. 31:29] If the children also are wicked, their sufferings are a punishment; [Ezek. 18:20, Prov. 3:12, Rom. 8:28] if they are godly, their sufferings are a chastening.

In the Next World God will punish by Exclusion from Heaven and from His Presence; [Matt. 22:13] and by Eternal Misery in Hell. [Rev. 21:8, Matt. 25:41]

II. BLESSING.

GOD PROMISES GRACE AND EVERY BLESSING. [Rom. 2:10+]

1. *To Whom?* TO ALL WHO KEEP THESE COMMANDMENTS. It is true, all men are sinners, and no one keeps these commandments perfectly. [Rom. 3:23+] But the godly try earnestly to keep them, [I Cor. 9:27] and are truly sorry for every failure to do so. [Rom. 7:24] To them, therefore, God promises grace and every blessing.

2. *Why?* God will bless them, not because they have earned a reward, but because He is merciful and gracious. [Ps. 103:11+, Joel 2:13] We cannot earn anything from God but punishment. His blessing is bestowed upon us solely as a gift of grace.

3. *How?*

In this World God blesses the godly with: Peace of Heart; [John 14:27] His Favor and Guidance; [Ps. 34:15+] True Success in Life; [Rom. 8:28] and a Blessed Hope of Salvation. [Rev. 2:10+]

Children and remote descendants share in the blessing of godly ancestors.

In the Next World God will grant them: Entrance into Heaven for Christ's Sake; [Matt. 25:34] and Eternal Glory and Blessedness. [John 14:2-3, Rev. 3:21]

A WARNING. An impenitent life will bring upon us God's punishment in time and eternity. WE SHOULD THEREFORE DREAD HIS DISPLEASURE, AND NOT ACT CONTRARILY TO THESE COMMANDMENTS.

AN ENCOURAGEMENT. A *godly life* will bring upon us God's blessing in time and eternity. WE SHOULD THEREFORE LOVE AND TRUST IN HIM, CHEERFULLY DO WHAT HE HAS COMMANDED US.

THE TEN COMMANDMENTS CONDEMN US; for we have broken them by thought, word, and deed. [John 1:8-10+, Rom 3:23, Eccl 7:20, Jas 2:10+]

We are not able to keep them perfectly. [Rom 7:18-19] Consequently we cannot be saved by them. [Gal 3:11] They are meant to show us our sinfulness, [Rom 3:20] to lead us to repentance, and to direct as to Christ for salvation. [Gal 3:24] We can be saved only through Him. [John 14:6+, Acts 4:12+] We are taught concerning Christ, and confess our faith in Him in the Second Part of the Catechism which now follows, namely, The Creed.

QUESTIONS.—1. What does God mean when He says that He is a jealous God? 2. Whom will God punish? 3. Why will He punish? 4. How does He punish? 5. To whom does God promise grace and blessing? 6. Why will He bless them? 7. How will He bless them? 8. What warning is contained in the Conclusion of the Commandments? 9. What encouragement is contained in it? 10. Why can we not be saved by the Ten Commandments? 11. What are the Commandments meant to do? 12. How only can we be saved? 13, Where are we taught concerning Christ?

SCRIPTURE VERSES.—Rom. 1:18. For the wrath of God is revealed from heaven against all ungodliness and unrighteousness of men, who hold the truth in unrighteousness.

Ezek. 18:4. The soul that sinneth, it shall die.

Rom. 6:23. For the wages of sin is death; but the gift of God is eternal life through Jesus Christ our Lord.

Gal. 6:7. Be not deceived; God is not mocked: for whatsoever a man soweth, that shall he also reap.

Gen. 18:25. Shall not the Judge of all the earth do right?

Heb. 12:6. Whom the Lord loveth he chasteneth.

Rom. 2:10. But glory, honour, and peace, to every man that worketh good; to the Jew first, and also to the Gentile.

Rom. 3:23. For all have sinned, and come short of the glory of God.

Ps. 103:11. For as the heaven is high above the earth, so great is his mercy toward them that fear him.

Ps. 34:1-5. The eyes of the LORD are upon the righteous, and his ears are open unto their cry.

Rev. 2:10. Be thou faithful unto death, and I will give thee a crown of life.

I John 1:8-9. If we say that we have no sin, we deceive ourselves, and the truth is not in us. If we confess our sins, he is faithful and just to forgive us our sins, and to cleanse us from all unrighteousness.

Jas. 2:10. For whosoever shall keep the whole law, and yet offend in one point, he is guilty of all.

John 14:6. Jesus saith unto him, I am the way, the truth, and the life: no man cometh unto the Father, but by me.

Acts 4:12. Neither is there salvation in any other: for there is none other name under heaven given among men, whereby we must be saved.

READING.—The Fall into Sin and its Punishment, Gen. 3.

ILLUSTRATIONS.—*Punishment*: Adam and Eve; Cain, Gen. 4:9-15; The Deluge, Gen. 6-8; Sodom and Gomorrah, Gen. 19; The Ten Plagues, Exod. 7-12; Korah, Numb. 16; Saul, I Sam. 15; The Assyrian and Babylonian Captivities, II Kings 17, II Kings 25. *Blessing*: Abraham, Gen. 12:2; Joseph, Gen. 45:4-8; David, II Sam. 7:16; Cornelius, Acts 4:10.

PART II.
THE CREED.

CHAPTER XV.
CREEDS OR CONFESSIONS.

THE CREED, from the Latin *Credo, I believe*, means that which we as Christians believe. The Creed given in our Catechism is the Apostles' Creed. It is so called, not because it was written by the apostles, but because it contains, in a brief summary, the doctrines which the apostles taught. It grew out of the words of the baptismal formula: "In the name of the Father and of the Son and of the Holy Ghost." [Matt 28:19] It has come down to us from the early centuries of the Church's history, and is *her confession of faith*. It should be our confession also; we should say from the heart, "I believe in God, etc." There are

Two KINDS OF CREEDS or Confessions of Faith:—

I. *Oecumenical* or Universal Creeds, which are accepted by the whole Christian Church throughout the world. They are

1. The Apostles' Creed.
2. The Nicene Creed.
3. The Athanasian Creed.

II. *Particular* Creeds or Confessions, which are accepted by the various Churches and Denominations as their distinctive confessions.

Our Lutheran Confessions are:—

1. The Augsburg Confession.
2. The Apology (Defense) of the Augsburg Confession.
3. The Schmalcald Articles.
4. The Small Catechism.
5. The Large Catechism.
6. The Formula of Concord.

These nine confessions together form the Book of Concord.

THE APOSTLES' CREED CONTAINS, in Three Articles, a statement of what the Triune God, the Father, the Son, and the Holy Ghost, has done and still does for us.

Article I. treats of God the Father and His work of *Creation*.

Article II. treats of God the Son and His work of *Redemption*.

Article III. treats of God the Holy Ghost and His work of *Sanctification*.

THE TRINITY. There is only one God, [Deut. 6:4] but there are three Persons, Father, Son, and Holy Ghost. Hence, we say that God is the Holy Trinity, or the Three in One. We cannot understand or explain how God can be three Persons and yet only one God. But we must not expect with our finite mind to comprehend the infinite God. We must accept the truth concerning God as He himself has revealed it to us in His Word. He plainly tells us that He is One; for He says, "*I am the Lord thy God; thou shalt have no other gods before Me*." [Exod. 20:2-3] Yet He also plainly tells us that there are three Persons. They are expressly mentioned in Christ's command to His disciples, "Go ye, and make disciples of all nations, baptizing them in the name of the Father and of the Son and of the Holy Ghost." [Matt. 28:19] And they were all revealed at the baptism of Jesus, when the Father spoke from heaven and said, "This is my beloved Son in whom I am well pleased," and the Holy Ghost descended on Jesus in the form of a dove. [Matt. 3:16-17] Each Person of the Holy Trinity has a share in the work of our salvation. The Father sent His Son to save us; [John 3:16] the Son became man and died for us; [Rom. 5:8] and the Holy Spirit applies redemption to our souls [I Cor. 12:3] through the Word of God and the Sacraments.

QUESTIONS.—1. Define the word Creed. 2. Why is the Apostles' Creed so called? 3. How did it originate? 4. What two kinds of creeds are there? 5. Name the oecumenical creeds. 6. Name the particular creeds or confessions of the Lutheran Church? 7. What does the Apostles' Creed contain? 8. Of what do the three articles of the Apostles' Creed treat? 9. What is meant by the Holy Trinity? 10. How do we know that God is only one God? 11. How do we know there are three Persons? 12. How do the three Persons of the Trinity share in the work of our salvation?

CHAPTER XVI.
THE FIRST ARTICLE.
OF GOD THE FATHER, OR CREATION.

I believe in God the Father Almighty, Maker of heaven and earth.

What is meant by this Article?

I believe that God has created me and all that exists; that He has given and still preserves to me my body and soul, with all my limbs and senses, my reason and all the faculties of my mind, together with my raiment, food, home and family, and all my property: that He daily provides me abundantly with all the necessaries of life, protects me from all danger, and preserves me and guards me against all evil; all which He does out of pure, paternal and divine goodness and mercy, without any merit or worthiness in me; for all which I am in duty bound to thank, praise, serve and obey Him. This is most certainly true.

I BELIEVE IN, that is, I trust in, I rely upon.

GOD THE FATHER, He is the Father of my Lord Jesus Christ, [Matt. 11:25] and the first Person of the Holy Trinity. Through Christ He is also my Father. [John 20:17, Eph. 1:3+]

ALMIGHTY, He is able to do all things, and to help me in every time of need.

MAKER OF HEAVEN AND EARTH. [Ps. 102:25] He has made all things,—the universe and all that it contains. The world did not come into being of itself or by chance, nor did it exist from eternity. God made it out of nothing. In the beginning He created the heaven and the earth. [Gen. 1:1+, Ps 33:6, 9] They were at first a formless mass; [Gen. 1:2] but in six days God fashioned the formless mass into the world as it now exists. On these six days He created, 1. Light, 2. The Firmament, 3. Land and Sea, 4. Sun, moon and stars, 5. Fishes and birds, 6. Beasts and man. [Gen 1:3-31]

God's Chief Creatures are the angels in heaven and men on earth. All His creatures, as they came from His hands, were very good. [Gen. 3:31] But some of the angels sinned, and became bad angels or devils. [II Pet. 2:4] And man also, though created in the image of God, fell into sin, and lost his original righteousness and holiness. [Gen. 3, Gen. 8:21, Eph. 4:24]

Luther's explanation of this Article in the catechism tells us:

I. What God has done and still does for me,

II. Why God does all this for me,

III. What I owe to God in return.

I. WHAT GOD HAS DONE AND STILL DOES FOR ME.
I BELIEVE THAT GOD HAS

1. CREATED ME [Job. 33:4+] AND ALL THAT EXISTS; [Neh. 9:6, Col. 1:16+] THAT HE HAS GIVEN TO ME

MY BODY,—WITH ALL MY LIMBS AND SENSES. Though my body, like that of the beasts, is made of the dust of the ground, [Gen. 2:7+] it is vastly superior to their bodies, and is a marvelous piece of divine workmanship, [Ps. 139:14] exquisitely adapted to be the earthly tabernacle of the soul which inhabits it.

MY SOUL, [Gen. 2:7+]—MY REASON AND ALL THE FACULTIES OF MY MIND, by which I am placed so far above the brute creation. God made the human soul to be a likeness of Himself; [Gen. 1:27, Gen. 9:6] that is, He gave to man in a limited measure those powers and faculties which He Himself possesses in unlimited and infinite measure. And while the human mind has become dimmed by the fall, its powers and faculties are still most wonderful.

2. PRESERVES ME. [Neh. 9:6] All that has helped to support my life has been God's gift; namely, MY RAIMENT, FOOD, HOME AND FAMILY, AND ALL MY PROPERTY. I continue to live because He sustains me. [Jas. 1:17+, Acts 17:28+]

HE DAILY PROVIDES ME ABUNDANTLY WITH ALL THE NECESSARIES OF LIFE. [Ps. 115:15-16+] His care for me is a constant, daily care. His mercies are new every morning. [Matt. 6:31-32+, Lam. 3:22-23+]

HE PROTECTS ME FROM ALL DANGER, SEEN AND UNSEEN. [Ps. 34:7, Matt. 10:30] I am beset with perils on every hand. If God withdrew His protecting hand, I should perish immediately.

HE PRESERVES ME AND GUARDS ME AGAINST ALL EVIL. [Ps 121:5, 8+] No real evil can come upon God's children. What seems an evil is meant for a good purpose, and is a blessing in disguise. [Rom. 8:28+, Isa. 55:8-9, Jer. 29:11, Ps. 23:4+]

II. WHY GOD DOES ALL THIS FOR ME.

He does it purely

1. OUT OF PATERNAL AND DIVINE GOODNESS AND MERCY. [Ps. 103:13+] It is

PATERNAL or fatherly [Ps 103:13+] goodness and mercy, because He is my Father through Jesus Christ, and loves me as His child. It is

DIVINE goodness and mercy, because God is love, [I John 4:16+] and only His unspeakable love could move Him to bestow His great benefits upon sinful men, even upon the wicked and unthankful. [Matt. 5:45+]

2. WITHOUT ANY MERIT OR WORTHINESS IN ME. [Gen. 32:10+] I have merited (deserved) nothing and I am worthy of nothing but punishment; for I am a sinful being, [Ps. 51:5] and I have broken God's law many times by thoughts and words and deeds. [Jer. 14:7]

III. WHAT I OWE TO GOD IN RETURN.

For all His goodness and mercy

I AM IN DUTY BOUND [Ps. 116:12+, Ps. 50:14]

1. TO THANK AND PRAISE HIM. I must not receive God's benefits as a matter of course, but must recognize them as gifts of His grace, and daily thank and praise Him in my heart and with my lips. [Ps. 103:1+]

2. TO SERVE AND OBEY HIM. I must show my gratitude in my life by obeying God's commandments and giving myself with all my heart to His service. [Rom. 12:1+]

THIS IS MOST CERTAINLY TRUE; namely, 1. That all the blessings I enjoy come from God, 2. That they are the gifts of His grace and that I am unworthy of them, 3. That I owe to God the fullest gratitude of heart and life.

QUESTIONS.—1. What does "I believe" mean? 2. Why do we say "God the *Father*"? 3. What does "Almighty" mean? 4. What has God made? 5. Name His chief creatures. 6. What three things does Luther's explanation of this article tell us? 7. What has God done and what does He still do for us? 8. In creating us, what has God given us? 9. How does He preserve us? 10. Why does God do all this for us? 11. Why are we not worthy of it? 12. What do we owe to God in return? 13. What is meant by thanking and praising Him? 14. What is meant by serving and obeying Him? 15. What is most certainly true according to this article?

SCRIPTURE VERSES.—Eph. 1:3. Blessed be the God and father of our Lord Jesus Christ, who hath blessed us with all spiritual blessings in heavenly places in Christ.

Gen. 1:1. In the beginning God created the heaven and the earth.

Job 33:4. The Spirit of God hath made me, and the breath of the Almighty hath given me life.

Col. 1:16. For by him were all things created, that are in heaven, and that are in earth, visible and invisible, whether they be thrones, or dominions, or principalities, or powers: all things were created by him, and for him.

Gen. 2:7. And the Lord God formed man of the dust of the ground, and breathed into his nostrils the breath of life; and man became a living soul.

Jas. 1:17. Every good gift and every perfect gift is from above, and cometh down from the Father of lights, with whom is no variableness, neither shadow of turning.

Acts 17:28. For in him we live, and move, and have our being.

Ps. 145:15, 16. The eyes of all wait upon thee; and thou givest them their meat in due season. Thou openest thine hand, and satisfiest the desire of every living thing.

Matt. 6:31, 32 Therefore take no thought, saying, What shall we eat? or, What shall we drink, or, Wherewithal shall we be clothed? (For after all these things do the Gentiles seek:) for your heavenly Father knoweth that ye have need of all these things.

Lam 3:22, 23. It is of the LORD'S mercies that we are not consumed, because his compassions fail not. They are new every morning.

Ps. 34:7. The angel of the LORD encampeth round about them that fear him, and delivereth them.

Ps. 121:5, 8. The LORD is thy keeper: the LORD is thy shade upon thy right hand. The LORD shall preserve thy going out and thy coming in from this time forth, and even for evermore.

Rom. 8:28. And we know that all things work together for good to them that love God, to them who are the called according to his purpose.

Ps. 23:4. Yea, though I walk through the valley of the shadow of death, I will fear no evil: for thou art with me; thy rod and thy staff they comfort me.

Ps. 103:13. Like as a father pitieth his children, so the Lord pitieth them that fear him.

I John 4:16. God is love; and he that dwelleth in love dwelleth in God, and God in him.

Matt. 5:45. He maketh his sun to rise on the evil and on the good, and sendeth rain on the just and on the unjust.

Gen. 32:10. I am not worthy of the least of all the mercies, and of all the truth, which thou hast shewed unto thy servant.

Ps. 116:12. What shall I render unto the LORD for all his benefits toward me?

Ps. 103:1. Bless the LORD, O my soul: and all that is within me, bless his holy name. Bless the LORD, O my soul, and forget not all his benefits.

Rom. 12:1. I beseech you therefore, brethren, by the mercies of God, that ye present your bodies a living sacrifice, holy, acceptable unto God, which is your reasonable service.

READING.—The Creation of the World, Gen. 1.

ILLUSTRATIONS.—*Provides*: Manna, Exod. 16:14; Elijah, I Kings 17:6, 14; Feeding the Five Thousand, Matt. 14:15-21. *Protects*: The Israelites, Exod. 14:19 *seq.*; Daniel, Dan. 6:22; Paul, Acts 22:12-33; Acts 27: 42-44. *Guards from evil*: Joseph; Job. *Thankfulness*: Noah, Gen. 8:20; The Samaritan, Luke 17:15,16.

CHAPTER XVII.
THE SECOND ARTICLE
OF GOD THE SON, OR REDEMPTION.

And in Jesus Christ His only Son our Lord; who was conceived by the Holy Ghost, born of the Virgin Mary; suffered under Pontius Pilate, was crucified, dead and buried; He descended into hell; the third day He rose again from the dead: He ascended into heaven, and sitteth on the right hand of God the Father Almighty; from thence He shall come to judge the quick and the dead.

What is meant by this Article?

I believe that Jesus Christ, true God, begotten of the Father from eternity, and also true man, born of the Virgin Mary, is my Lord; who has redeemed me, a lost and condemned creature, secured and delivered me from all sins, from death and from the power of the devil, not with silver and gold, but with His holy and precious blood, and with His innocent sufferings and death, in order that I might be His, live under Him in His kingdom, and serve Him in everlasting righteousness, innocence, and blessedness, even as He is risen from the dead, and lives and reigns to all eternity. This is most certainly true.

The Second Article treats of Jesus Christ, THE SON OF GOD, and his work of REDEMPTION. Prompted by His infinite love, God pitied our lost race, and determined to save us by sending a Redeemer in the person of His only Son. [John 3:16+, I Tim. 1:15+] Throughout the centuries of Old Testament history He repeatedly gave the promise of redemption: In Eden, [Gen. 3:15] to the patriarchs, [Gen. 12:3, Gen. 26:4] to David, [II Sam. 7:12-13] and through the prophets. [Isa. 9:2-7, Mic. 5:2] In the fulness of time God seat His Son into the world. [Gal. 4:4]

Article II. and its Explanation may be analyzed as follows:—

I. OUR LORD.

1. *His Names*: Jesus, Christ.
2. *His Person and Nature*: True God and True Man.
3. *His Life*: His Humiliation and His Exaltation.

II. HIS WORK OF REDEMPTION.

1. *Whom He has redeemed.*
2. *From what He has redeemed me.*
3. *How He has redeemed me.*
4. *Why He has redeemed me.*

OUR LORD.
I. HIS NAMES.
I BELIEVE THAT

JESUS. This was our Lord's personal name, given to Him by the angel. [Matt. 1:21] It signified, "He shall save."

CHRIST. This was His official name, corresponding with the Old Testament name "Messiah," [John 1:41] and signified "The Anointed One." God anointed Him with the Holy Spirit for the work of redemption, [Luke 4:18-21] to a threefold office:—

    1. As Prophet, to teach us God's will. [Acts 3:22]

    2. As Priest, to atone for our sins, and to intercede for us. [Heb. 4:14]

    3. As King, [Matt. 21:5, Rev. 17:14] to reign over us in the Kingdom of Power, of Grace, and of Glory.

II. HIS PERSON AND NATURE.

He is

TRUE GOD, BEGOTTEN OF THE FATHER FROM ETERNITY. Christ is true God, [Rom. 9:5+] just as the Father is God. [John 5:23+, John 20:28+, John 8:58+, Mat. 16:16] He is the Son of God, not as a good or great man who has been received or adopted as God's son, but He is in His very nature the Son of God, *begotten by His Father* [John 3:16+] *from all eternity*. [John 1:1, John 17:5] He is "God of God, Light of Light, Very God of Very God, Begotten, not made, being of one substance with the Father." [John 10:30+] The Scriptures show this by ascribing to Him divine names, attributes, power, honor, and works. At His baptism and at His transfiguration the Father spoke from heaven, and said, "This is my beloved Son, in whom I am well pleased." [Matt. 3:17, Matt. 17:5] His divine nature is proved by His teaching, His miracles, His holy life, and especially by His resurrection from the dead.

ALSO TRUE MAN, BORN OF THE VIRGIN MARY. Christ was in all respects a human being such as we are, except that He was without sin. [I Pet. 2:22+] He was "conceived by the Holy Ghost," and thus had God alone for His Father. [Luke 1:35] But He was "born of the Virgin Mary," [Luke 2:7] with a human body [Heb. 2:14] and soul. [Matt. 26:38] He grew, increased in wisdom and stature, [Luke 2:52] and reached the age of manhood. He suffered our human wants, [Matt. 4:2, John 4:6-7] such as hunger, thirst, weariness, and pain. He was moved by human emotions, [Luke 10:21, Matt. 26:38, Matt. 21:12] such as joy, sorrow, and indignation. He wept, [John 11:35] prayed, [Matt. 26:39] suffered, and died. [I Pet. 2:23-24] He could not have done these things if He had not been true man.

Christ is therefore both God and man in one Person. [Rom. 1:3-4, John 1:14+] Consequently He is the *God-Man*. It was necessary that the Redeemer should be both God and man. [I Tim. 1:15+] If He had not been God, but only man, He could not have paid a sufficient ransom for our deliverance from sin, nor have acquired any merit to bestow upon us. Even a sinless man could have saved no one but himself. On the other hand, if Christ had not become man, but remained God only, He could not have put Himself in our place under the law, nor have suffered and died in our stead. But as the *God-man*, Christ was able to accomplish, and did perfectly accomplish, our redemption. [Rom. 3:24+] Thus He became and

IS MY LORD, WHO HAS REDEEMED ME, and in whom I trust for salvation. [Rom. 8:38-39, Rom. 5:1+]

QUESTIONS.—1. Of what does the Second Article treat? 2. How did God plan to save man? 3. Analyze the Second Article and its Explanation. 4. Give the meaning of the names of our Lord. 5. What was Christ's threefold office? 6. What is to be said about the person and nature of Christ? 7. In what sense is Christ the Son of God, and how do we know it? 8. How do you know that Christ was true man? 9. Why was it necessary that the Redeemer should be both God and man? 10. What name do we give to Christ in view of His two-fold nature?

SCRIPTURE VERSES.—John 3:16. For God so loved the world, that he gave his only begotten Son, that whosoever believeth in him should not perish, but have everlasting life.

I Tim. 1:15. This is a faithful saying, and worthy of all acceptation, that Christ Jesus came into the world to save sinners; of whom I am chief.

Rom. 9:5. Christ came, who is over all, God blessed for ever.

John 5:23. That all men should honour the Son, even as they honour the Father. He that honoureth not the Son honoureth not the Father which hath sent him.

John 20:28. And Thomas answered and said unto him, My Lord and my God.

John 8:58. Jesus said unto them, Verily, verily, I say unto you, Before Abraham was, I am.

John 10:30. I and my Father are one.

I Pet. 2:22. Who did no sin, neither was guile found in his mouth.

John 1:14. And the Word was made flesh, and dwelt among us, (and we beheld his glory, the glory as of the only begotten of the Father,) full of grace and truth.

Rom. 3:24. Being justified freely by his grace through the redemption that is in Christ Jesus.

Rom. 5:1. Therefore being justified by faith, we have peace with God through our Lord Jesus Christ.

READING.—The Birth of Jesus, Luke 2:1-20; or, The Eternal Word, John 1:1-18.

CHAPTER XVIII.
OUR LORD.
III. HIS LIFE.

The Saviour's life includes two states; namely, His Humiliation and His Exaltation.

HIS HUMILIATION.

Christ's state of humiliation comprises His life on earth, during which He laid aside the full use of His divine glory and was content to appear among men in the form of a servant. He humbled Himself, and became obedient unto death, even the death of the cross, [Phil. 2:8+] in order that He might redeem us. He gave men glimpses of His divine glory: in the authority with which He taught, [Matt. 7:28-29] in the holy life which He led, [John 8:46] and in the miracles which He performed. [John 2:11] But in general He appeared like other men.

This state of humiliation includes five stages:—He was

1. CONCEIVED BY THE HOLY GHOST, BORN OF THE VIRGIN MARY. Christ might have appeared among men in the full splendor of His divine glory and majesty. But, in order to redeem us, He was content to be born in poverty, [Luke 2:7, II Cor. 8:9+, Matt. 8:20+] to grow up in obscurity, [Matt. 2:23] and to appear to most men as if He were simply a man.

2. SUFFERED UNDER PONTIUS PILATE. The whole life of Jesus on earth was a life of suffering endured for our sakes. He bore all the trials and hardships which have come upon our race as a result of its sinfulness. He also suffered constant persecution at the hands of his enemies. [Heb. 12:3; John 1:11] But His greatest sufferings came at the end of His life, in the agony of Gethsemane, [Matt. 26:36-46] in the mock-trial before the Jewish Council, [Matt. 26:57-75] and in His sufferings under Pontius Pilate, the Roman governor. [Matt. 27:1-30] He was mocked, spitefully entreated, spitted on, crowned with thorns, and scourged; and then He

3. WAS CRUCIFIED. [Luke 23:33] Though innocent and holy, He was treated as though He were a malefactor, and was put to a cruel and shameful death. He was nailed to a cross, and left suspended there till He died. So great was His agony, that He cried out, "My God, my God, why hast Thou forsaken me?" [Mark 15:34]

4. DEAD. After unspeakable sufferings, Jesus died on the cross. [Mark 15:37] He was really, and not seemingly, dead. [John 19:33-34] He voluntarily gave up His life for ours. [John 10:18-19+] His death was *vicarious*. He suffered the penalty for our sins. [I Pet. 3:18, Isa. 53:5+]

5. BURIED. His body was laid away in the grave, where our bodies shall decay. But since Christ was "the Holy One of God," His body could not "see corruption." [Ps. 16:10]

HIS EXALTATION.

After the work of redemption was completed, Christ assumed the full use of the glory and majesty which had belonged to Him as the Son of God from eternity; His human nature was exalted to a full share in the glory of His divine nature. [Phil. 2:9-11+] He had humbled Himself as a man; and He was exalted as a man. His divine nature, being unchangeable, can neither be humbled nor exalted. [Heb. 13:8]

Christ's exaltation, like His humiliation, includes five stages:—

1. HE DESCENDED INTO HELL. Immediately before His resurrection He descended into the place of the departed spirits and proclaimed His victory. [I Pet. 3:19]

2. THE THIRD DAY HE ROSE AGAIN FROM THE DEAD. Having paid in full the penalty for our sins, He rose again from the dead, triumphant, on the third day (Easter). He had power to lay down His life, and power to take it again. [John 10:19] As His death had been a real death, so His resurrection was a real resurrection. He reappeared to His disciples, not as a spirit, but with the same body that was crucified, the prints of the nails and of the spear being plain in His hands and side. [Luke 24:36-40] But His body was a transformed and glorified body, with new properties and powers. [John 20:19]

The Resurrection a Fact. The reality of the resurrection is established beyond all doubt. The strongest proof of its reality is found in the fact that the disciples themselves were so unwilling to believe it, but were obliged to do so by the evidence of their own senses. Even the doubting Thomas exclaimed, "My Lord, and my God." [John 20:28] During the forty days between His resurrection and His ascension the Lord gave His disciples so many proofs of His resurrection that all their doubts were removed. [Acts 1:3] The women on Easter morn found the grave empty and were told by an angel that He had risen. [Mark 16:6] He was seen by Mary in the Garden, [John 20:14-16] by Peter, [Luke 24:34] by the two disciples at Emmaus, [Luke 24:15] twice by the eleven as they were gathered together, [John 20:19-29] by seven disciples at the Sea of Tiberias, [John 21:1] by more than five hundred brethren at once, [I Cor. 15:6] by James, [I Cor. 15:7] and by the eleven when He accompanied them to Mount Olivet and ascended before their eyes to heaven. [Acts 1:9-12] The wonderful change which took place in the apostles when the risen and ascended Christ had sent the Holy Spirit upon them, [Acts 2] and the wonderful change which took place in Paul, [Acts 9:1-29] are further proofs of the reality of the resurrection of Christ.

The Resurrection proves 1. That Jesus is the Son of God. [John 20:28, Rom. 1:4+, Acts 2:36] 2. That the sacrifice which He made for sin was sufficient and accepted. [Rom. 8:34, I Thess. 1:10] 3. That we also shall rise from the dead. [Rom. 4:25+, I Cor. 15:19-20+, I Cor. 6:14]

3. HE ASCENDED INTO HEAVEN from Mount Olivet forty days after His resurrection. [Acts 1:9] Having finished His work on earth, He returned to the heaven from which He had come. He has gone to prepare a place for us. [Acts 14:2]

4. AND SITTETH ON THE RIGHT HAND OF GOD THE FATHER ALMIGHTY; that is, on the right hand of God's power. As the God-man He now wields all power in heaven and earth. [Matt. 28:18+, Eph. 1:20-22+] He rules over all creatures in the realm of Power; over the believers in the realm of Grace (the Church on earth); and over angels and saints in the realm of Glory in heaven. He continues His office of Highpriest, and intercedes for us with the Father. [Rom. 8:34+, Heb. 4:14-16]

5. FROM THENCE HE SHALL COME TO JUDGE THE QUICK AND THE DEAD. At the end of the world Christ will come again visibly, [Mark 13:26+] suddenly, and unexpectedly, [Matt. 24:36-42, Luke 21:27] with power and great glory, to judge both the quick (living) and the dead. [II Cor. 5:10+, Matt. 25:31-46] He will separate the believing from the unbelieving; receive the believers unto Himself; and cast the impenitent and unbelieving into outer darkness and torment. His coming will fill the believers with joy, [Luke 21:28] and the unbelievers with dismay. [Rev. 6:15-17] No one knows or can compute the exact time of His coming. We should be always ready. [Matt. 24:42, 44+] His coming will be preceded by signs. [Luke 21:25-26] The present order of the world shall pass away; [II Pet. 5:10] and there shall be new heavens and a new earth, wherein dwelleth righteousness. [II Pet. 3:13+]

QUESTIONS.—1. What two states does Christ's life include? 2. What is meant by His state of humiliation? 3. How many stages were there in His humiliation? 4. Name them. 5. Was Christ's glory entirely hidden during his state of humiliation? 6. How might Christ have appeared, and how did He appear among men? 7. Describe the sufferings of Christ? 8. What is to be said of Christ's crucifixion? 9. What is to be said of Christ's death? 10. What is to be said of His burial? 11. What is meant by Christ's exaltation? 12. How many stages were there in His exaltation? 13. Name them. 14. What is meant by the descent into hell? 15. How did Christ re-appear to His disciples? 16. Prove that the resurrection was a fact. 17. What does the resurrection of Christ prove? 18. When and why did Christ ascend into heaven? 19. What is meant by His sitting at the right hand of the Father? 20. What can you tell about Christ's second coming?

SCRIPTURE VERSES.—Phil. 2:8. And being found in fashion as a man, he humbled himself, and became obedient unto death, even the death of the cross.

II Cor. 8:9. For ye know the grace of our Lord Jesus Christ, that, though he was rich, yet for your sakes he became poor, that ye through his poverty might be rich.

John 10:18, 19. Therefore doth my Father love me, because I lay down my life, that I might take it again. No man taketh it from me, but I lay it down of myself.

Isa. 53:5. He was wounded for our transgressions, he was bruised for our iniquities: the chastisement of our peace was upon him; and with his stripes we are healed.

Phil. 2:9-11. Wherefore God also hath highly exalted him, and given him a name which is above every name: that at the name of Jesus every knee should bow, of things in heaven, and things in earth, and things under the earth; and that every tongue should confess that Jesus Christ is Lord, to the glory of God the Father.

Heb. 13:8. Jesus Christ, the same yesterday, and to-day, and for ever.

Rom. 1:4. Declared to be the Son of God with power, according to the spirit of holiness, by the resurrection from the dead.

Rom. 4:25. Who was delivered for our offences, and was raised again for our justification.

I Cor. 15:19, 20. If in this life only we have hope in Christ, we are of all men most miserable. But now is Christ risen from the dead, and become the firstfruits of them that slept.

Matt 28:18. And Jesus came and spake unto them, saying, All power is given unto me in heaven and in earth.

Eph. 1:22. And hath put all things under his feet.

Rom. 8:34. Who is he that condemneth? It is Christ that died, yea rather, that is risen again, who is even at the right hand of God, who also maketh intercession for us.

Mark 13:26. And then shall they see the Son of man coming in the clouds with great power and glory.

II Cor. 5:10. For we must all appear before the judgment seat of Christ; that every one may receive the things done in his body, according to that he hath done, whether it be good or bad.

Matt. 24:44. Therefore be ye also ready: for in such an hour as ye think not the Son of man cometh.

II Pet. 3:13. Nevertheless we, according to his promise, look for new heavens and a new earth, wherein dwelleth righteousness.

READING.—The Death and Resurrection of Christ, Luke 23-24:9; and The Ascension of Christ, Acts 1:1-11.

CHAPTER XIX.
CHRIST'S WORK OF REDEMPTION.
I. WHOM HE HAS REDEEMED.

He HAS REDEEMED

ME. Christ died for all; [I Pet. 2:24+, I John 2:2+, John 1:29+] and consequently for me also. [Gal. 2:20+] Believing on Him, all the blessings of His redemption belong to me In time and in eternity. He is *my* Saviour, *my*Redeemer.

A LOST AND CONDEMNED CREATURE. I was lost, [Isa. 53:6+, I Pet. 2:25] because my sin had separated me from God, and I could not have found my way back to Him, if Christ had not sought and found me. I was condemned, [Eph. 2:3] because I had broken God's commandments and deserved eternal punishment.

II. FROM WHAT HE HAS REDEEMED ME.

He has SECURED AND DELIVERED ME

FROM ALL SINS; namely, from the *guilt* of sin by paying its penalty for me on the cross; [I John 1:7, II Cor. 5:21+] and from the *dominion* of sin by giving me grace to fight against it and overcome it. [Rom 6:14, Rom. 8:2-4]

FROM DEATH: not from bodily death, for even the Christian must die; but from the fear of bodily death; [Phil. 1:23, I Cor. 15:55, 57] from spiritual death; [Eph. 2:6] and from everlasting death. [John 3:16]

AND FROM THE POWER OF THE DEVIL. [I John 3:8+] On account of my sins, I was in Satan's power. But Christ has freed me. Since He has paid the penalty for my sins, Satan no longer has any claim upon me, and can no longer harm me. [John 10:27-28] He still tempts me to sin; but Christ gives me grace to resist. He still accuses me before God on account of my sins; but Christ shields me against Satan's accusations by the satisfaction which He, my Saviour, has made for all my sins. [I John 2:1]

III. HOW HE HAS REDEEMED ME.

NOT WITH SILVER AND GOLD; [I Pet. 1:18, 19+] for no material wealth could purchase freedom from spiritual slavery and death. Nor has He redeemed me merely by becoming my great teacher and example; for this would not take away my guilt;

BUT WITH HIS HOLY AND PRECIOUS BLOOD. [I John 1:7+] His blood was the price which Christ paid for my ransom. It was holy, because He was holy; and precious, because He was the Son of God. The shedding of Christ's blood for my sins was the only way in which I could be redeemed; for without the shedding of blood, there is no remission of sins. [Heb. 9:22]

AND WITH HIS INNOCENT SUFFERINGS [I Pet. 3:18+] AND DEATH. [Rom. 5:7-8+] Christ suffered and died, not for any sins of His own, but for *my* sins. He was innocent and had no sin at all. But He voluntarily bore the punishment which I deserved, and thus satisfied all the demands of divine justice for me. Since He has borne the punishment for me, I, believing on Him, need no longer be punished.

Christ was my Substitute. By His holy life He perfectly fulfilled God's law in my place; [Rom 5:19] and by His innocent sufferings and death He bore the punishment for my sins in my place. [II Cor. 5:21+] All that Christ has done is imputed to me by faith; [Rom. 4:24] that is, it is all counted as if I myself had done it. [Rom. 4:5] His death, therefore, frees me from guilt and condemnation; and His holy life makes me appear righteous In God's sight and fit to enter into heaven. My entire hope of salvation rests on Christ and what He has done for me. [II Cor. 5:19]

IV. WHY HE HAS REDEEMED ME.
IN ORDER THAT

I MIGHT BE HIS. He desired me for His own, and therefore purchased me with His precious blood. [II Cor. 5:15+] Hence I now belong to Him, and not to Satan or to myself. He wishes me to yield myself fully to Him in heart and life. [Gal. 2:20+] If I refuse to do so, I am withholding what belongs to Him.

LIVE UNDER HIM IN HIS KINGDOM; namely, in His kingdom of Grace on earth by a life of faith, and in His kingdom of Glory in heaven. [Col. 1:12-14]

AND SERVE HIM IN EVERLASTING RIGHTEOUSNESS, INNOCENCE AND BLESSEDNESS.

EVEN AS HE IS RISEN FROM THE DEAD, AND LIVES AND REIGNS TO ALL ETERNITY.

THIS IS MOST CERTAINLY TRUE: 1. That Jesus Christ, true God and true Man, is my Lord, who has redeemed me. 2. That He has paid the penalty for my sins with His holy and precious blood and His innocent sufferings and death. 3. That consequently I belong to Him, and should serve Him now and for ever.

QUESTIONS.—1. What four things does the explanation of the second article tell us about Christ's redemption? 2. Whom has Christ redeemed? 3. What was I before Christ redeemed me, and why? 4. From what has Christ redeemed me? 5. What is meant by redemption from sin? from death? and from the devil? 6. How has Christ redeemed me? 7. Why was the shedding of Christ's blood necessary? 8. Why did Christ suffer and die if He was innocent? 9. What is meant when we say that Christ was our substitute? 10. Why has Christ redeemed me? 11. To whom do I now belong, and what is my duty therefore? 12. What is meant by living under Christ in His kingdom? 13. In what spirit am I to serve Him? 14. What hope has Christ secured for me? 15. What three things are most certainly true according to this second article?

SCRIPTURE VERSES.—I Pet. 2:24. Who his own self bare our sins in his own body on the tree, that we, being dead to sins, should live unto righteousness: by whose stripes ye were healed.

I John 2:2. And he is the propitiation for our sins: and not for ours only, but also for the sins of the whole world.

John 1:29. Behold the Lamb of God, which taketh away the sin of the world.

Gal. 2:20. I live by the faith of the Son of God, who loved me, and gave himself for me.

Isa. 53:6. All we like sheep have gone astray.

II Cor. 5:21. For he hath made him to be sin for us, who knew no sin; that we might be made the righteousness of God in him.

I John 3:8. For this purpose the Son of God was manifested, that he might destroy the works of the devil.

I Pet. 1:18, 19. Forasmuch as ye know that ye were not redeemed with corruptible things, as silver and gold, from your vain conversation received by tradition from your fathers; but with the precious blood of Christ, as of a lamb without blemish and without spot.

I John 1:7. The blood of Jesus Christ his Son cleanseth us from all sin.

I Pet. 3:18. For Christ also hath once suffered for sins, the just for the unjust, that he might bring us to God.

Rom. 5:7, 8. For scarcely for a righteous man will one die: yet peradventure for a good man some would even dare to die. But God commendeth his love toward us, in that, while we were yet sinners, Christ died for us.

II Cor. 5:15. He died for all, that they which live should not henceforth live unto themselves, but unto him which died for them, and rose again.

Gal. 2:20. I am crucified with Christ: nevertheless I live; yet not I, but Christ liveth in me: and the life which I now live in the flesh I live by the faith of the Son of God, who loved me, and gave himself for me.

I Pet. 2:9. But ye are a chosen generation, a royal priesthood, a holy nation, a peculiar people; that ye should shew forth the praises of him who hath called you out of darkness into his marvellous light.

Matt. 16:24. Then said Jesus unto his disciples, If any man will come after me, let him deny himself, and take up his cross, and follow me.

READING.—Jesus our High Priest, Heb. 9:11-15.

CHAPTER XX.
THE THIRD ARTICLE
OF GOD THE HOLY GHOST, OR SANCTIFICATION

I believe in the Holy Ghost; the Holy Christian Church, the Communion of Saints; the Forgiveness of sins; the Resurrection of the Body; and the Life Everlasting. Amen.

What is meant by this article?

I believe that I cannot by my own reason or strength believe in Jesus Christ my Lord, or come to Him; but the Holy Ghost has called me through the Gospel, enlightened me by His gifts, and sanctified and preserved me in the true faith; in like manner as He calls, gathers, enlightens, and sanctifies the whole Christian Church on earth, and preserves it in union with Jesus Christ in the true faith; in which Christian Church He daily forgives abundantly all my sins, and the sins of all believers, and will raise up me and all the dead at the last Day, and will grant everlasting life to me and to all who believe in Christ. This is most certainly true.

THE THIRD ARTICLE treats of GOD THE HOLY GHOST and His work of SANCTIFICATION. It tells us how we become partakers of the Redemption which is described in the Second Article. Christ *has accomplished* our redemption, and the Holy Ghost *applies* that redemption to our souls. The work of the Holy Ghost *in* us is as necessary for our salvation as the [Cor. 2:14] work of Christ *for* us. We must believe in Christ, if we would be saved; [Mark 16:16] and it is the Holy Ghost who causes us to believe. [1 Cor. 12:3]

Article. III, and its Explanation may be analyzed as follows:—

THE HOLY GHOST,

I. *His Person and Nature*: He is True God.

II. *His Work*: He Calls, Enlightens, Sanctifies, and Preserves me in the true Faith.

III. *His Workmanship*: The Holy Christian Church.

IV. *The Fruits of His Work*: 1. The Forgiveness of Sins. 2. The Resurrection of the Body, and the Life Everlasting.

THE HOLY GHOST.
I. HIS PERSON AND NATURE.

I BELIEVE IN THE HOLY GHOST. The Holy Ghost is true God. He is not simply a power or energy of God, but a Person. [Acts 5:3-4] "He proceedeth from the Father and the Son, and with the Father and the Son together is worshipped and glorified." [John 14:26, John 15:26] The Scriptures ascribe to Him divine names, attributes, power, honor, and works. Christ commanded His disciples to baptize men in the name of the Father and of the Son *and of the Holy Ghost*. [Matt. 28:19]

The Holy Spirit instructed the prophets and teachers of Old Testament times, [II Peter 1:21] and was poured out upon the apostles on the day of Pentecost. [Acts 2] He inspired the Holy Scriptures. [II Tim. 3:16] He comes into our hearts through the Word of God and the Sacraments.

II. HIS WORK.

The work of the Holy Ghost is *Sanctification*. This word is used here, at the head of the Third Article, in the wide sense, and includes the Holy Spirit's entire work upon our souls; namely, Calling, Enlightening, Sanctification in the narrower sense, and Preservation in the Faith.

1. ITS NECESSITY. If the Holy Spirit does not work in us, we cannot be saved. Hence, we say in the catechism,

I BELIEVE THAT I CANNOT BY MY OWN REASON OR STRENGTH BELIEVE IN JESUS

2. ITS NATURE. BUT THE HOLY GHOST HAS

CALLED ME THROUGH THE GOSPEL. [II Tim. 1:9] He has caused His Word to be written [II Thess. 2:14, II Tim. 3:16] and causes it to be continually proclaimed [John 20:31+, II Cor. 5:20, I Cor. 1:21] for the purpose of making God's grace known to me, and inviting me to share in it. He calls all men, and means His call earnestly. He does not merely seem to call some, but actually calls all who hear or read His Word. [I Tim. 2:4+, I Pet. 3:9] And along with the call, He gives us the strength which we need in order to believe. [Eph. 2:4-6] Those who obey the call are the Elect or Chosen [Matt. 20:16] ones, and obtain salvation. Those who refuse to obey the call are lost. [Mark 16:16]

ENLIGHTENED ME BY HIS GIFTS. The Holy Ghost shows me my lost condition and God's saving mercy, and thus leads me to Repentance through the Law, [John 16:8, Rom. 3:20] and to Faith through the Gospel. [John 15:26, John 1:17]

Repentance includes

1. An Acknowledgment and Confession of Sin. [Ps. 51:3, 4]

2. Sincere Sorrow for Sin. [Luke 22:62] It must be sorrow for the sin itself, and not merely for the consequences of sin.

3. The Hating and Forsaking of Sin. [Ps. 51:10]

4. An Earnest Desire for Forgiveness. [Ps. 51:2, 9]

True repentance always leads to faith. [II Cor. 7:10] Sorrow for sin which does not lead to faith, is not repentance but remorse, and often drives men to despair. [Matt. 27:3-5]

Faith includes

1. A Knowledge of the Facts of the Gospel. [Rom. 10:14]

2. A Belief of the Facts. [Rom. 4:20, 21]

3. Trust or Confidence in Christ our Saviour. [II Tim. 1:12+] This trust is the chief part of faith.

True faith is not a mere matter of the head, but of the heart. It is not a mere intellectual belief that God exists or that Christ lived and died; but it is a firm confidence that Christ is actually *our* Saviour, and that all *our* sins are washed away by His precious blood. Faith says, "The Son of God loved [I John 1:7] me, and gave Himself *for me.*" [Gal. 2:20]

True faith is always preceded by repentance. The impenitent have no promise of forgiveness, and therefore cannot have faith. They cannot believe a promise which has not been given to them.

Regeneration and Conversion. Those whom the Holy Spirit has brought to repentance and faith are in a state of regeneration and conversion. The change which has taken place in them is called a new birth or regeneration, [John 3:5, 6] because a new life has been planted in them. [II Cor. 5:17+] It is called conversion, [Acts 3:19] because they have been converted or turned from sin to righteousness, from self to God.

It is not necessary that a Christian should be able to point to the exact time of his conversion. The important question is not, "When were we converted?" but, "Are we now in a converted state?" that is, "Are we now penitent and believing?"

Justification. All those who have true faith are justified: [Rom. 5:1+, Rom. 4:5] their sins are forgiven, and the righteousness of Christ is imputed (counted as belonging) to them. [Phil. 3:9] When we believe in Christ, all that He has done and suffered for us is regarded by God as if we had done and suffered it ourselves; [II Cor. 5:21, Rom. 8:1+] for Christ was our substitute. Consequently, those who believe in Christ are *justified* for His sake; that is, they are pronounced by God to be righteous and fit to enter into heaven.

By Faith Alone. We are justified and saved by faith alone, without works. [Rom. 3:28+] We shall enter heaven, not because we deserve to enter, [Gal. 2:16+] but only because we believe in Christ. Salvation is a *Gift*: acquired for us by Christ's holy life and innocent death; bestowed upon us freely by God's grace; and accepted by faith. [Eph. 2:8, 9+] Our faith is not a merit on account of which we are forgiven, but it is the hand with which we reach out and accept the free gift of forgiveness which God offers for Christ's sake.

Our own works have nothing to do with our justification. [Rom. 3:20+] If God took them into consideration at all, they would condemn us; for at best we are imperfect and sinful creatures. [Rom. 7:18-23, Gal. 3:10+] In order to be saved, we need a *perfect* righteousness, Christ's righteousness alone is perfect. It becomes ours by faith.

AND SANCTIFIED. Those who have true faith are sanctified by the Holy Spirit; that is, they are made holy in heart and life. [Rom. 8:5+, Rom. 6:22] While good works do not save us, they do and must follow faith as its fruit. [Matt. 7:18] Believers should do good works out of love to God and gratitude for His mercy. Faith that does not result in a holy life is a dead faith, [Jas. 2:26+] and cannot save. The Christian dare not live in sin. [Rom. 6:2+] He has become a new creature; for he is born again: and consequently he leads a new life. We shall, indeed, never become sinless in this world, but we must honestly and earnestly *try* to do God's will in all things. [Phil. 3:12-14, Matt. 5:16+] We should grow more and more holy every day. [Eph. 4:22-24, Rom. 12:2, I Thess. 4:1] We cannot do this by our own power, but we can by the help of God. We should, therefore, be diligent and faithful in the use of the Word of God and the Sacraments; for these are the means which the Holy Ghost uses for our sanctification.[4]

[Footnote 4: Faith in Christ does not at once make us perfectly holy and sinless, as some persons maintain; but it takes away the guilt of our sin. We are completely justified and forgiven as soon as we believe; but we are not completely sanctified. Sanctification is a gradual process, which will be completed only when we are transformed and glorified in heaven.]

PRESERVED ME IN THE TRUE FAITH. As it is the Holy Ghost who brings us to faith, so it is He who preserves us in it. [Phil. 1:6+] The world, the flesh, and the devil are enemies who seek to destroy our faith and to rob us of our salvation. We should constantly pray for strength to resist these enemies, [Matt. 26:41+, Rev. 2:10] and should obey the promptings of the Holy Spirit. We must avoid wilful, intentional sin, [Eph. 4:30+] and live a life of daily repentance. If we sin wilfully, we fall from grace and are lost, unless we come to true and lasting repentance. If we faithfully use the Means of Grace, and earnestly strive to lead a Christian life, the Holy Spirit will preserve us in the faith to the end. [Phil. 2:12, 13+]

QUESTIONS.—1. Of what does the Third Article treat? 2. What is to be said about the importance of the Holy Spirit's work? 3. Analyze the Third Article and its Explanation. 4. What is to be said about the person and nature of the Holy Ghost? 5. How does the Holy Ghost come into our hearts? 6. Describe the Work of the Holy Ghost. 7. Why can we not be saved if the Holy Spirit does not work in us? 8. How has the Holy Spirit called me? 9. How has He enlightened me? 10. How does the Holy Ghost bring me to repentance? 11. What does repentance include? 12. How does the Holy Ghost bring me to faith? 13. What does faith include? 14. What is true faith? 15. What is meant by regeneration? 16. What is meant by conversion? 17. Must a Christian know the exact time of his conversion? 18. What is meant by justification? 19. What is the relation of faith and works in salvation? 20. What is meant by sanctification? 21. What is the relation between faith and good works? 22. How are we preserved in the faith?

SCRIPTURE VERSES.—I Cor. 2:14. But the natural man receiveth not the things of the Spirit of God: for they are foolishness unto him: neither can he know them, because they are spiritually discerned.

John 20:31. But these are written, that ye might believe that Jesus is the Christ, the Son of God; and that believing ye might have life through his name.

I Tim. 2:4. Who will have all men to be saved, and to come unto the knowledge of the truth.

Matt. 20:16. So the last shall be first, and the first last: for many be called, but few chosen.

II Tim. 1:12. For I know whom I have believed, and am persuaded that He is able to keep that which I have committed unto him against that day.

II Cor. 5:17. Therefore if any man be in Christ, he is a new creature: old things are passed away; behold, all things are become new.

Rom. 5:1. Therefore being justified by faith, we have peace with God through our Lord Jesus Christ.

Rom. 8:1. There is therefore now no condemnation to them which are in Christ Jesus.

Rom. 3:28. Therefore we conclude that a man is justified by faith without the deeds of the law.

Gal. 2:16. Knowing that a man is not justified by the works of the law, but by the faith of Jesus Christ.

Eph. 2:8, 9. For by grace are ye saved through faith; and that not of yourselves: it is the gift of God: not of works, lest any man should boast.

Rom. 3:20. Therefore by the deeds of the law there shall no flesh be justified in his sight: for by the law is the knowledge of sin.

Gal. 3:10. For as many as are of the works of the law are under the curse: for it is written, Cursed is every one that continueth not in all things which are written in the book of the law to do them.

Rom. 8:5. For they that are after the flesh do mind the things of the flesh; but they that are after the Spirit, the things of the Spirit.

Jas. 2:26. For as the body without the spirit is dead, so faith without works is dead also.

Rom. 6:2. God forbid. How shall we, that are dead to sin, live any longer therein?

Matt. 5:16. Let your light so shine before men, that they may see your good works, and glorify your Father which is in heaven.

Phil. 1:6. Being confident of this very thing, that he which hath begun a good work in you will perform it until the day of Jesus Christ.

Matt. 26:41. Watch and pray, that ye enter not into temptation: the spirit indeed is willing, but the flesh is weak.

Eph. 4:30. And grieve not the Holy Spirit of God, whereby ye are sealed unto the day of redemption.

Phil. 2:12, 13. Work out your own salvation with fear and trembling; for it is God which worketh in you both to will and to do of his good pleasure.

READING.—The Outpouring of the Holy Ghost, Acts, 2:1-41.

ILLUSTRATIONS.—*Calling*: The Great Supper, Luke 14:16-24; The Marriage of the King's Son, Matt. 22; Matthew, Matt. 9:9; Peter and Andrew, Matt. 4:19; Nathanael, John 1:45. *Repentance*: David, Ps. 51; Peter, Luke 22:62; Zaccheus, Luke 19; The Prodigal Son, Luke 15:11-24; The Publican, Luke 18:13. *Impenitence*: Cain, Gen. 4:13; Judas, Matt. 27:4, 5; The Pharisee, Luke 18:10-12, *Faith*: The Centurion, Matt. 8:5-13; The Woman of Cana, Matt. 15:22-28; Peter, John 6:68, 69. *Doubt*: Thomas, John 20:22-28. *Conversion*: The Twelve Disciples; The Three Thousand, Acts 2; The Thief on the Cross, Luke 23:39-43; The Philippian Jailor, Acts 16:25-34.*Faithfulness*: Paul, II Cor. 11:23-33; II Tim. 4:7. *Apostasy*: Ananias, Acts 4:5; Demas, II Tim. 4:10.

CHAPTER XXI.
THE HOLY GHOST.
III. HIS WORKMANSHIP.
The Holy Christian Church, the Communion of Saints.

WHAT THE CHURCH IS. The Church is "The Communion of Saints" or fellowship of believers. It consists of all those persons who truly believe in Christ. [Matt. 16:16, 18] We call it the *Workmanship* of the Holy Ghost, because He brings men to faith and thus produces the Church. HE CALLS, GATHERS, ENLIGHTENS AND SANCTIFIES THE WHOLE CHRISTIAN CHURCH ON EARTH, AND PRESERVES IT IN UNION WITH JESUS CHRIST IN THE TRUE FAITH. [Eph. 3:25-27]

The Church may also be called the Holy Spirit's *Workshop*, because He abides and works in it through the Means of Grace,—the Word of God and the Sacraments.

WHEN FOUNDED. The Holy Christian Church was founded on the day of Pentecost, when the Holy Ghost was poured out upon the disciples. [Acts 2:1-41] On that day the Gospel of the crucified and risen Saviour was first preached by the apostles, the first converts were made, and the first Christian baptisms were administered.

VISIBLE OR INVISIBLE. The Church is invisible, because we cannot read men's hearts nor tell who are real believers. But if we regard the Church as an external organization which includes all who profess to believe, it is visible. In this outward visible Church there are many persons who are not real believers. But Christ knows His own. [II Tim 2:19+, John 10:14+] The angels on the day of judgment will separate the hypocrites from the true Christians. [Matt. 13:41, 42]

THE MARKS OF THE CHURCH. The Church is found wherever the Gospel is rightly taught and the Sacraments are rightly administered. For wherever God's Word is preached, some persons believe it, [Isa. 55:10, 11] and where believers are, there is the Church.

THE CHURCH IS ONE. It consists of the true believers out of all the different churches, denominations, and sects. There is one Flock, with one Shepherd. [John 10:16] The Church is the Body of which Christ is the Head. [Col. 1:18, Eph 1:22, 23]

ITS NAMES. The Church is called *Holy*, because the Holy Spirit works in it and through it, and because its members, though not perfect, lead holy lives. It is called *Christian*, because it consists of those who believe in Christ. It is called *Catholic* or Universal, because it is meant to include all men everywhere. Catholic does not mean *Roman* Catholic.

MILITANT AND TRIUMPHANT. The Church, consisting of true believers, is one and the same Church on earth and in heaven. On earth it is the Church Militant, because its members are still fighting the good fight of faith. [I Tim. 6:12+] In heaven it is the Church Triumphant, because its members have won the victory of faith. [Rev. 7:9-14, Rev. 2:18, Rev. 3:21] The only way into the Church Triumphant is through the Church Militant.

THE CHURCH'S WORK.

The Church is the agency or instrument which the Holy Spirit uses for the evangelization of the world. [Matt. 28:19, Mark 16:15] It is the institution through which He does His work of applying redemption to the souls of men. The Church, therefore, has a work to do: namely, to make disciples of all men.

THE MEANS through which the Church, as an agency of the Holy Spirit, is to do its work are the Word of God and the Sacraments. They are sufficient for the purpose for which they are intended, because the Holy Spirit works through them and endows them with supernatural power. [Rom. 1:16, Heb. 4:12]

THE WORKMEN who are to preach the Word and administer the Sacraments are the *ministers*. They must be properly called and ordained by the Church. [Act 14:23, Tit. 1:5] In the New Testament all pastors are called elders or bishops. It was only at a later period that the office of a bishop was made superior to that of elder, pastor or minister. The office of an apostle was a separate and higher office. The apostles were the witnesses of Christ's redemption, and possessed miraculous powers. They have no successors. Ministers are the ambassadors of Christ, beseeching men to be reconciled to God. [II Cor. 5:20+] Christ speaks through them. He who hears them, hears Christ; he who despises them, despises Christ. [Luke 10:16] If a minister should happen to be a hypocrite, his official acts, such as baptisms and the like, would still be valid. [II Tim. 2:13] *Deacons* [Acts 6:1-6] are officers whose duty it is to assist the pastor, and to look after the temporal interests of the congregation.*Deaconesses* [Rom.16:1] are consecrated to the work of love and mercy, and minister to the sick, the needy, the neglected, the ignorant, the fallen, and the friendless.

THE VARIOUS CHURCHES.

While the Church, in the strict sense of the word, is the "communion of saints" and therefore *one*, yet outwardly it has become divided, in the course of time, into many different churches, denominations, and sects. It contains Four Great Branches: *The Greek Catholic Church*; *The Roman Catholic Church*; *The Evangelical Lutheran Church*; and *The Reformed Churches*, comprising a great number of denominations and sects. The Lutheran Church and the Reformed Churches are called Protestant. (For the names and relations of various branches of the Church, see the accompanying Diagram, on page 106.)

THE EVANGELICAL LUTHERAN CHURCH.

The Evangelical Lutheran Church is in reality the old original Church which came into existence on the day of Pentecost. Luther simply threw out the errors which had crept into the Church during the course of the centuries, and held fast the doctrines taught in God's Word. As a separate and distinct Church, the Lutheran Church dates from the year 1530, when the Augsburg Confession was read before the emperor and diet of the German Empire.[5] Her doctrines are laid down in her six Confessions, contained in the Book of Concord.

[Footnote 5: Since a particular Church is no older than her distinctive confession, the Lutheran Church is more than thirty years older than the Roman Catholic Church; for the Augsburg Confession was adopted in 1530, while the Canons and Decrees of the Council of Trent, which are the Confession of the Roman Catholic Church, were not completed until 1563. The ecumenical creeds are accepted by both Churches, and therefore prove nothing as regards their *relative* age.]

THE CHURCH OF THE PURE GOSPEL. The Lutheran Church receives the Holy Scriptures of the Old and New Testaments as the only rule and standard of religious teaching. The Roman Catholic Church accepts the tradition of the Church as of equal authority with the Holy Scriptures.

The Lutheran Church teaches the great central doctrine of the Gospel, that we are saved by *faith alone* without works. The Roman Catholic Church teaches that we are justified by faith *and works*.

The Lutheran Church abides by the teachings of Scripture even when she cannot understand them. The other Protestant Churches explain away and reject some teachings of Scripture because they cannot understand them.

HER NAME. The name Lutheran was first given to our Church by her enemies. But she accepted it, because she believes the doctrines which Luther taught. The name which she chose for herself is Evangelical (true to the Gospel). She is now known by both names taken together, Evangelical Lutheran.

WHERE FOUND. The Lutheran Church is found in nearly all parts of the world, especially in Germany, Scandinavia, and the United States. In 1905 she numbered over 73 million baptized members, or practically as many as all the other Protestant Churches taken together. In the United States she has almost two million confirmed members (statistics for 1906), and ranks third in size among the Protestant Churches of the country.

IN AMERICA. The Lutheran Church in North America comprises the following general bodies: The General Synod, organized in 1821; the General Council, organized in 1867; the Synodical Conference, organized in 1872; the United Synod South, organized in 1886. To these general bodies there belong various synods. There are also a number of Independent Synods which are not connected with any general body. Synods are often subdivided into Conferences.

HER WORK. The Lutheran Church, like the Church in general, is to make disciples (Christians) of men. She is all the more bound to do her work, because she is the Church of the Pure Gospel. Her work is done in local congregations, in Home Missions, Foreign Missions, Inner Missions, and in maintaining the necessary institutions of learning (colleges, seminaries, etc.) and of mercy (orphanages, asylums, hospitals).

DUTIES OF HER MEMBERS. It is the duty of her members to lead a Christian life, to be loyal to their own Church, and to co-operate heartily in all her local and general work, for the glory of God and the salvation of immortal souls.

QUESTIONS.—1. What is the Christian Church? 2. Why do we call it the Workmanship of the Holy Ghost? 3. When was it founded? 4. Is the Church visible or invisible? 5. What are the marks of the Church? 6. Why is the Christian Church one? 7. Why is the Church called Holy, Christian, Catholic? 8. What is meant by the Church Militant and the Church Triumphant? 9. What use does the Holy Spirit make of the Church? 10. What are the means which the Church uses for its work? 11. Who are the Church's workmen, and what is their work? 12. Name the four great branches of the Christian Church? 13. How old is the Lutheran Church? 14. What three fundamental principles characterize the Lutheran Church? 15. Explain how the Lutheran Church got its name. 16. Where is the Lutheran Church found? 17. How large is it? 18. Name the General Bodies of the Lutheran Church in North America. 19. Describe the work of the Lutheran Church? 20. What are the duties of her members?

SCRIPTURE VERSES.—Matt. 16:18. Upon this rock I will build my church; and the gates of hell shall not prevail against it.

II Tim. 2:19. Nevertheless the foundation of God standeth sure, having this seal, The Lord knoweth them that are his. And, Let every one that nameth the name of Christ depart from iniquity.

John 10:14. I am the good shepherd, and know my sheep, and am known of mine.

Eph. 1:22, 23. And hath put all things under his feet, and gave him to be the head over all things to the church, which is his body, the fulness of him that filleth all in all.

I Tim. 6:12. Fight the good fight of faith, lay hold on eternal life, whereunto thou art also called, and hast professed a good profession before many witnesses.

Rom. 1:16. For I am not ashamed of the gospel of Christ: for it is the power of God unto salvation to every one that believeth.

Heb. 4:12. For the word of God is quick, and powerful, and sharper than any two-edged sword, piercing even to the dividing asunder of sold and spirit, and of the joints and marrow, and is a discerner of the thoughts and intents of the heart.

II Cor, 5:20. Now then we are ambassadors for Christ, as though God did beseech you by us: we pray you in Christ's stead, be ye reconciled to God.

READING.—The Church at Jerusalem, Acts 2:41-47.

CHAPTER XXII.
THE HOLY GHOST.
IV. THE FRUITS OF HIS WORK.

The Forgiveness of Sins; the Resurrection of the Body; and the Life Everlasting.

The fruits of the Holy Spirit's work in us are: 1. The Forgiveness of Sins. 2. The Resurrection of the Body and the Life Everlasting.

1. *THE FORGIVENESS OF SINS* has been acquired for me by my Saviour Jesus Christ; [I John 1:7+] but it is made mine by the Holy Ghost, who has brought me to faith and preserved me in it. For it is through faith that I obtain forgiveness. [Rom 5:1]

IN WHICH CHRISTIAN CHURCH. The forgiveness of sins is made mine *in the Church* through the Word of God and the Sacraments. Faith takes hold of and clings to the promises therein given. Special assurance of forgiveness is also given in Confession and Absolution.

HE DAILY FORGIVES ABUNDANTLY ALL MY SINS. Even if I am a sincere Christian, I am an imperfect and sinful creature, and I need God's forgiveness every day. [I John 1:8, 9, Rom. 7:18-25] By keeping me in a state of repentance and faith, the Holy Spirit secures to me the continuous forgiveness of all my sins. The Christian's life is a daily repentance and a daily believing that God for Christ's sake graciously pardons all our transgressions and shortcomings. [Luke 11:3, 4, Rom 8:32+]

AND THE SINS OF ALL BELIEVERS. All who lead a life of daily repentance and faith are daily and abundantly forgiven.

2. *THE RESURRECTION OF THE BODY AND THE LIFE EVERLASTING.* The work of the Holy Spirit in me will not be completed until the last day.

HE WILL RAISE UP ME AND ALL THE DEAD AT THE LAST DAY. The bodies of all men shall be raised from the dead and re-united with the souls from which they were parted at death. [John 5:28, 29+, Acts 24:15+] These bodies will be essentially the same which we had on earth, but they will be immortal and incorruptible. [I Cor. 15:42] The bodies of the believers will be endowed with new and glorious properties, like the body of Christ after His resurrection. [I Cor. 15:42-44, Phil. 3:21+] They will be fit tabernacles for the glorified souls to inhabit through all eternity. They will be spiritual bodies, freed from all the imperfections and limitations to which they were subject on earth. The bodies of those believers who are still alive at Christ's second coming shall undergo the same change in a moment, in the twinkling of an eye, at the last trump. [I Cor. 15:51-53]

AND WILL GRANT EVERLASTING LIFE TO ME TO ALL WHO BELIEVE IN CHRIST.

Eternal Death. The impenitent and unbelieving shall be cast into eternal torment, [Matt. 25:41] and shall suffer indescribable pain and misery for ever. [Rev. 14:11] The greater their wickedness and neglected opportunities on earth, the deeper will be their remorse and anguish. [Luke 12:47, 48, Matt. 25:41] Having refused to let the Holy Spirit make them fit for entrance into heaven, [Rev. 21:27, Matt. 7:23] they shall be cast out into the only place for which they are fit, into hell. [Luke 16:23, 24]

QUESTIONS.—1. What are the fruits of the Holy Spirit's work in us? 2. How does the forgiveness of sins become yours? 3. Where is the forgiveness of sins made yours? 4. How do we obtain daily forgiveness? 5. When will the Holy Spirit's work in you be completed? 6. Describe the resurrection of the dead. 7. What is to be said about everlasting life? 8. Why will the impenitent and unbelieving be cast into hell?

SCRIPTURE VERSES.—I John 1:7. The blood of Jesus Christ his Son cleanseth us from all sin.

Rom. 8:32. He that spared not his own Son, but delivered him up for us all, how shall he not with him also freely give us all things?

John 5:28, 29. Marvel not at this: for the hour is coming, in the which all that are in the graves shall hear his voice, and shall come forth; they that have done good, unto the resurrection of life; and they that have done evil, unto the resurrection of damnation.

Acts 24:15. There shall be a resurrection of the dead, both of the just and unjust.

Phil. 3:21. Who shall change our vile body, that it may be fashioned like unto his glorious body, according to the working whereby he is able even to subdue all things unto himself.

I Pet. 1:4. To an inheritance incorruptible, and undefiled, and that fadeth not away, reserved in heaven for you.

Rev. 21:4. And God shall wipe away all tears from their eyes; and there shall be no more death, neither sorrow, nor crying, neither shall there be any more pain: for the former things are passed away.

READING.—Christ Judging the World, Matt. 25:31-46.

PART III.
THE LORD'S PRAYER.

CHAPTER XXIII.
PRAYER.

Prayer is the conversation of the believing heart with God. [Ps. 19:14+] It is as necessary for the life of the soul, as breathing is for that of the body. As children of God we must live in communion with Him; and we cannot be Christians without prayer. For this reason God has given us His name to use in prayer, and the Saviour has taught us how to pray in the Lord's Prayer.

To WHOM WE SHOULD PRAY. Our prayers should be addressed to God alone, [Matt. 4:10.] and not to the Virgin Mary, the saints, the angels, or any other creatures.

WHY WE SHOULD PRAY. We should pray, 1. Because we constantly need God's mercy in temporal and spiritual things. 2. Because we owe God our thanks for his many benefits. [Ps. 103, Jas. 1:17] 3. Because God has commanded us to pray. [Matt. 6:9, Matt. 26:41] 4. Because God has promised to hear us. [Matt. 7:7, 8+, Ps. 50:15]

WHEN WE SHOULD PRAY. 1. Always; [Luke 21:36+] that is, our soul should live in constant communion with God, and always be open toward Him. 2. Whenever we feel special need of prayer: in danger, [Matt. 8:25] distress, anxiety, [Matt. 8:25] sickness, [Jas. 5:14, 15] bereavement, sorrow, [Ps. 25:16, 17] temptation, [Matt. 26:41] or when we are burdened with the sense of our guilt. [Luke 18:13.] 3. At fixed times: [Dan. 6:10] every morning and evening, at meal-times; in family worship; [Josh. 24:15+] in church. [Matt. 18:20+]

FOR WHOM WE SHOULD PRAY. 1. For ourselves. 2. For our fellow-Christians. [Eph. 6:18+] 3. For all men: [I Tim. 2:1+] for friends and foes, [Matt. 5:44+] the poor and the rich, the afflicted and the tempted. 4. For the Church. 5. For the State.

OUR PRAYERS SHOULD CONTAIN: 1. Adoration, 2. Thanksgiving. 3. Confession, 4. Petition. 5. Intercession.

THE MANNER. Our prayers should be the sincere utterance of our hearts; otherwise they will be a mere mockery. [Matt. 6:5] They may be in our own words or those of another. It will often be profitable to use the prayers found in good prayer-books or in the Liturgy, and to draw largely from the Psalms, which are a treasury of good and beautiful prayers. We should not lengthen our prayers by vain repetitions, nor repeat the Lord's Prayer or any other prayer a certain number of times as if that were a merit. [Matt. 6:7] Nor should we shorten our prayers through laziness, indifference, and the like. The Lord's Prayer should generally be added to our own prayers as a summary of those things for which we should pray.

THE POSTURE which we assume should indicate reverence to God. We should kneel or stand with folded hands. If we are unable to assume either of these postures, we may pray in any position. We stand in church on Sunday, because it is the day of the Lord's resurrection and a day of joy. We should not sit still in church while others stand, unless we are too weak or ill to stand. Kneeling is an attitude of humiliation, particularly appropriate for the confession of sins.

IN CHRIST'S NAME. We should always pray in Christ's name, and never omit His name to please men or avoid offence; for our prayers are only heard for Christ's sake. We have the promise that whatever we ask in His name will be given to us. [John 16:23] To pray in Christ's name means to pray, 1. As one who trusts in Christ and asks to be heard for His sake. [Eph. 2:18+, Rom. 5:2] 2. As one who prays in Christ's spirit, submitting all things to God's will, and saying with Christ, "Not my will, but Thine, be done." [Matt. 26:29, Matt 6:10]

IN FAITH. We should pray in faith, believing that God will answer our prayer for Jesus' sake. [Jas. 5:16+] If we do not pray in faith, we shall not be heard. [Jas. 1:6, 7]

THE ANSWER TO PRAYER. God always answers the prayer of the believer. Those who ask and receive not, have either asked amiss, [Jas. 4:3] or have not asked in faith. If we ask anything according to His will, He heareth us. [John 5:14+] He answers our prayer, 1. By granting us what we ask, though perhaps after a long delay, by which He tries our faith and patience. 2. He grants us good things instead of the hurtful things for which we ignorantly ask. 3. He gives us strength to bear the burden which we pray to have removed, [II Cor. 12:9] and thus confers a greater blessing than the removal of the burden would be.

QUESTIONS.—1. What is prayer? 2. To whom alone should we pray? 3. Why should we pray? 4. When should we pray? 5. For whom should we pray? 6. What should our prayers contain? 7. What is to be said about the manner of our praying? 8. What is to be said about the posture in prayer? 9. Why must we pray in Christ's name? 10. What is meant by praying in Christ's name? 11. What is to be said about the importance of praying in faith? 12. Does God always answer prayer? 13. In what ways does He answer?

SCRIPTURE VERSES.—Ps. 19:14. Let the words of my mouth, and the meditation of my heart, be acceptable in thy sight, O Lord, my strength, and my redeemer.

Matt. 7:7, 8. Ask, and it shall be given you; seek, and ye shall find; knock, and it shall be opened unto you. For everyone that asketh receiveth, and he that seeketh findeth; and to him that knocketh it shall be opened.

Luke 21:36. Watch ye, therefore, and pray always, that ye may be accounted worthy to escape all these things that shall come to pass, and to stand before the Son of man.

Josh. 24:15. As for me and my house, we will serve the LORD.

Matt. 18:20. For where two or three are gathered together in my name, there am I in the midst of them.

Eph. 6:18. Praying always with all prayer and supplication in the Spirit, and watching thereunto with all perseverance and supplication for all saints.

I Tim. 2:1, 2. I exhort, therefore, that, first of all, supplications, prayers, intercessions, and giving of thanks be made for all men; for kings, and for all that are in authority; that we may lead a quiet and peaceable life in all godliness and honesty.

Matt. 5:44. Pray for them which despitefully use you, and persecute you.

Eph. 2:18. For through him we both have access by one Spirit unto the Father.

Jas. 5:16. The effectual fervent prayer of a righteous man availeth much.

I John 5:14. And this is the confidence that we have in him, that, if we ask anything according to his will, he heareth us.

II Cor. 12:9. And he said unto me, My grace is sufficient for thee: for my strength is made perfect in weakness.

READING.—The Pharisee and the Publican in the Temple, Luke 18:10-14.

ILLUSTRATIONS.—*Prayer for Self*: The Lepers, Luke 17:12, 13; The Blind Beggar, Luke 18:35-43; The Publican, Luke 18:13; *For Others*: Jesus, John 17, Luke 23:32; Abraham, Gen. 18:23-33; Moses, Exod. 32:11; Stephen, Acts 7:60. *Answer to Prayer*: Israel in Bondage, Exod. 2:23, 24; Hannah, I Sam. 1:9-20; Elijah, I Kings 17:21, 22; Jas. 5:17; The Early Church, Acts 12:5-17; Paul, Acts 16:25; I Cor. 12:7-9.

CHAPTER XXIV.
THE LORD'S PRAYER.

The Lord's Prayer is so-called because it was given to us by the Lord Jesus Christ. [Matt. 6:9-13, Luke 11:1-4] It teaches us how to pray aright, and is the model after which we should fashion all our prayers. It shows us the manner in which we should come to God, and the things for which we should ask.

ITS CONTENTS. The Lord's Prayer contains an Introduction, Seven Petitions, and a Conclusion. The first three petitions regard God's glory, and deal with His Name, His Kingdom, and His Will; the last four regard our bodily and spiritual needs, and deal with our Daily Bread, Forgiveness, Temptation, and Deliverance from Evil. Six petitions, the first three and the last three, refer to spiritual gifts; and only one, the fourth, refers to earthly gifts. Thus we are taught that, when we pray, we should think first of God's glory; and that we should pray more for spiritual than for temporal benefits.

INTRODUCTION.

Our Father Who art in Heaven.

What is meant by this Introduction?

God would thereby affectionately encourage us to believe that He is truly our Father, and that we are His children indeed, so that we may call upon Him with all cheerfulness and confidence, even as beloved children entreat their affectionate parent.

This Introduction shows us the manner in which we should come to God in prayer; namely, as His children, who are asking their Father for what they need, and who are sure that He loves them and will answer their prayer.

OUR FATHER.[6] God is our Father and we are His children through Christ our Saviour. [Gal 3:26+, 1 John 3:1, 2, Rom. 8:16] We should therefore be sure that He will receive us kindly for Jesus' sake whenever we come before him with our prayers. We should CALL UPON HIM WITH ALL CHEERFULNESS AND CONFIDENCE, EVEN AS BELOVED CHILDREN ENTREAT THEIR AFFECTIONATE PARENT. [Matt. 7:11+, Rom. 8:15+, Heb. 4:16]

[Footnote 6: Observe how the name "Father," by which we are here taught to address God, corresponds with the duty "to fear, love, and trust in Him above all things" as enjoined by the First Commandment.]

We are taught to say *our* and not *my* Father, because the Lord's Prayer was given to believers to use in their common worship as well as in their private devotions; and because we should pray not only for ourselves but for our fellow-believers and for all men.

WHO ART IN HEAVEN. An earthly father is not always able to do what his children ask, even if he desires to do so. But the Father to whom we here pray is our Heavenly Father, and is abundantly able to answer all our prayers, [Eph. 3:20+] He not only loves us with an everlasting love, but is almighty, omniscient, and all-wise. He is able to do all things which He wills to do, and will answer all our prayers in the very way that is best for us.

QUESTIONS.—1. Why is the Lord's Prayer so called? 2. What does it teach us? 3. What does it contain? 4. What can you say about the seven petitions? 5. What does the introduction show? 6. Why do we say Our *Father*? 7. How should this encourage us to call upon Him? 8. Why do we say *Our* Father? 9. What is to be said about our heavenly Father in comparison with earthly fathers?

SCRIPTURE VERSES.—Gal. 3:26. For ye are all the children of God by faith in Christ Jesus.

Matt. 7:11. If ye then, being evil, know how to give good gifts unto your children, how much more shall your Father which is in heaven give good things to them that ask him?

Rom. 8:15. For ye have not received the spirit of bondage again to fear; but ye have received the Spirit of adoption, whereby we cry, Abba, Father.

Eph. 3:20. Now unto him that is able to do exceeding abundantly above all that we ask or think, according to the power that worketh in us, unto him be glory in the church by Christ Jesus throughout all ages, world without end. Amen.

READING.—Christ teaches His Disciples to pray, Luke 11:1-4.

CHAPTER XXV.
THE FIRST PETITION.

Hallowed be Thy name.

What is meant by this Petition?

The name of God is indeed holy in itself; but we pray in this petition that it may be hallowed also by us.

How is this effected?

When the Word of God is taught in its truth and purity, and we, as the children of God, lead holy lives in accordance with it; to this may our blessed Father in heaven help us. But whoever teaches and lives otherwise than as God's Word prescribes, profanes the name of God among us; from this preserve us, heavenly Father.

In this Petition we pray for grace to hallow God's name[7] by the pure teaching of His Word and by childlike obedience to it.

[Footnote 7: There is a parallel between this Petition and the Second Commandment. We here pray for grace to avoid what the Second Commandment forbids, and to do what it commands.]

THE NAME OF GOD means not only the names by which we address Him, but all by which He is known to us. Compare the Second Commandment.

IS INDEED HOLY IN ITSELF. [Ps. 99:3] God's name is holy, because He is holy. We cannot increase or diminish God's holiness by anything that we do. This petition does not imply, therefore, that we are to *make* God's name holy.

BUT WE PRAY IN THIS PETITION THAT IT MAY BE HALLOWED ALSO BY US. We hallow God's name when we regard and treat it as holy; in other words, when we honor and glorify God by worshiping and serving Him in accordance with the revelation which He has given of Himself in His Word. [John 17:6+, Ps. 100:2, 3]

I. HOW GOD'S NAME IS HALLOWED.

1. WHEN THE WORD OF GOD IS TAUGHT IN ITS TRUTH AND PURITY. God has revealed Himself to us in His Word, and it is only from that Word that we can learn to know Him and worship Him aright. [John 1:18+] Those, therefore, who in the Church, the school, or the home, teach God's Word, as well as those who gladly hear, read, and learn it, hallow His name. [John 17:17+] But the Word must be taught in its truth and purity; that is, it must be taught as it is recorded in the Scriptures, with nothing added, taken away, or changed. [Gal. 1:9, Rev 22:18, 19]

AND WE AS THE CHILDREN OF GOD LEAD HOLY LIVES IN ACCORDANCE WITH IT. In order to hallow God's name, we must not only hear but obey His Word. [Jas. 1:22+, Matt. 5:16] As God's children we should think, speak, and act according to the rule which He has laid down in His Word, and thus glorify His name.

TO THIS MAY OUR BLESSED FATHER IN HEAVEN HELP US. We cannot preserve God's Word in its truth and purity against its foes, nor believe and obey it by our own strength: hence we pray for God's help.

II. HOW GOD'S NAME IS PROFANED.

BUT WHOEVER TEACHES AND LIVES OTHERWISE THAN AS GOD'S WORD PRESCRIBES,

FROM THIS PRESERVE US, HEAVENLY FATHER. We pray thus, because we are by nature inclined to error and sin, and have need of God's grace to preserve us from profaning His name.

QUESTIONS.—1. What do we pray for in this first petition? 2. What does the name of God mean? 3. Why is God's name holy in itself? 4. What does it mean to hallow God's name? 5. How is God's name hallowed? 6. Why do we pray for God's help? 7. How is God's name profaned? 8. Why do we pray God to preserve us from profaning His name?

SCRIPTURE VERSES.—John 17:6. I have manifested thy name unto the men which thou gavest me out of the world.

John 1:18. No man hath seen God at any time; the only begotten Son, which is in the bosom of the Father, he hath declared him.

John 17:17. Sanctify them through thy truth: thy word is truth.

Jas. 1:22. But be ye doers of the word, and not hearers only, deceiving your own selves.

READING.—The Name of Jesus, Acts 4:1-21.

CHAPTER XXVI.
THE SECOND PETITION.

Thy kingdom come.

What is meant by this Petition?

The kingdom of God comes indeed of itself without our prayer; but we pray in this petition that it may come unto us also.

When is this effected?

When our heavenly Father gives us His Holy Spirit, so that by His grace we believe His holy Word, and live a godly life here on earth and in heaven forever.

In this Petition we pray that the Kingdom of God may come to us[8] and to all men; that is, that we all by true faith and a godly life may become members of the Church on earth and in heaven.

[Footnote 8: Since the Kingdom of God comes to us through the Gospel, there is a close relation between this Petition and the Third Commandment, which commands us to "deem God's Word holy and willingly hear and learn it."]

THE KINGDOM OF GOD is the Kingdom which Christ has founded, and to which all who believe in Him belong. It is the Kingdom of Grace in this world and the Kingdom of Glory in the next. [Mark 1:15, Matt. 25:34]

COMES INDEED OF ITSELF WITHOUT OUR PRAYER. Christ has established His kingdom and will continue to extend it, whether we pray for it or not. [Isa. 9:7]

BUT WE PRAY IN THIS PETITION THAT IT MAY COME TO US ALSO; that is, into our hearts. In other words, we pray that we may become true Christians; [Matt. 7:21] and if we are Christians, we pray that we may become better Christians.

Missions. This petition is also a prayer for missions. [Matt. 9:37, 38+, Mark 16:15] We here pray that God's kingdom may come to all men. If our prayer is sincere, then we must be willing also to give liberally, so that the Gospel may be preached to the heathen (Foreign Missions) and to the spiritually destitute in our own land (Home Missions and Inner Missions).

HOW GOD'S KINGDOM COMES TO US.

WHEN OUR HEAVENLY FATHER GIVES US HIS HOLY SPIRIT. Since only believers belong to God's kingdom, and we "cannot by our own reason or strength believe in Jesus Christ our Lord," we pray in this petition that God would give His Holy Spirit to us,

SO THAT BY HIS GRACE WE BELIEVE HIS WORD, [I Cor. 12:3] AND LIVE A GODLY LIFE [Tit. 2:11-13+] HERE ON EARTH AND IN HEAVEN FOREVER. The Holy Spirit must teach us to repent of sin and to believe in Christ, and preserve us in a life of daily repentance and faith. Then God's kingdom will come to as more and more in this world, and in the next world we shall belong to it for ever.

QUESTIONS.—1. What do we pray in this petition? 2. What is meant by the kingdom of God? 3. How does God's kingdom come without our prayer? 4. What do we mean when we pray that it may come to us? 5. What is to be said about this petition and missions? 6. How does God's kingdom come to us? 7. Why do we need the Holy Spirit?

SCRIPTURE VERSES.—Matt. 9:37, 38. Then saith he onto his disciples, The harvest truly is plenteous, but the labourers are few; Pray ye therefore the Lord of the harvest, that he will send forth labourers into his harvest.

Mark 16:15. And he said unto them, Go ye into all the world, and preach the gospel to every creature.

Tit. 2:11-13. For the grace of God that bringeth salvation hath appeared to all men, teaching us that, denying ungodliness and worldly lusts, we should live soberly, righteously, and godly, in this present world, looking for that blessed hope, and the glorious appearing of the great God and our Saviour Jesus Christ.

READING.—The Harvest and the Laborers, Matt. 9:35-38.

CHAPTER XXVII.
THE THIRD PETITION.

Thy will be done on earth as it is in heaven.

What is meant by this Petition?

The good and gracious will of God is done, indeed, without our prayer, but we pray in this petition that it may be done by us also.

When is this effected?

When God frustrates and brings to nought every evil counsel and purpose which would hinder us from hallowing the name of God and prevent His kingdom from coming to us,—such as the will of the devil, of the world, and of our own flesh; and when he strengthens us and keeps us steadfast in His Word and in the faith even unto our end. This is His gracious and good will.

In this Petition we pray for grace gladly to believe, do, and suffer all that God wills us to believe, do, and suffer, so that His name may be hallowed, and His kingdom may come.

THY WILL. God's will is, 1. That we should believe the Gospel and be saved. [I Tim 2:4+] 2. That we should obey His commandments and be holy. [I Thess. 4:3+] 3. That we should willingly submit to all His dealings with us, and suffer patiently when He lays a cross on us. [Rom. 8:17+]

BE DONE ON EARTH AS IT IS IN HEAVEN. We pray that God's will may be done by all men and especially by us, as heartily, as continually, and as completely as it is done by the holy angels. [Ps. 103:20, 21]

THE GOOD AND GRACIOUS WILL OF GOD. The will of God is always good and gracious, because He always wills those things which He, in His wisdom and love, [I John 4:16] sees are best. He does all things well, even when we do not understand His ways. [Isa. 55:8, 9, Rom. 8:28]

IS DONE INDEED WITHOUT OUR PRAYER. There will always be some persons who permit God to accomplish His good and gracious purposes in them, whether we pray for it or not. [Isa. 55:11]

BUT WE PRAY IN THIS PETITION THAT IT MAY BE DONE BY US ALSO; [Rom. 12:12] that is, that we may believe His Gospel, obey His Commandments, and trustfully permit Him to lead us in whatsoever paths He will.

WHAT WE PRAY GOD TO DO.

In order that God's good and gracious will may be done by us, all opposing wills must be overcome. [Luke 22:31] We therefore pray God

1. TO FRUSTRATE AND BRING TO NOUGHT THE WILL OF THE DEVIL, [II Cor. 2:11] OF THE WORLD [I John 2:15, 16] (wicked persons), AND OF OUR OWN FLESH [Gal. 5:17+] (our natural heart). For these are the great enemies of our souls, who by their EVIL COUNSELS AND PURPOSES WOULD HINDER US FROM HALLOWING THE NAME OF GOD AND PREVENT HIS KINGDOM FROM COMING TO US. They tempt us to oppose God's will by despising His Gospel, disobeying His Commandments, and murmuring against His dealings with us. We pray God

2. TO STRENGTHEN US, [Phil. 2:13] so that we may be able to overcome these enemies and do God's will in spite of them. [Eph. 6:11, 12+] They are very powerful, but if we are in earnest about overcoming them, God will give us the needful strength in answer to our prayer. We pray God

3. TO KEEP US STEADFAST IN HIS WORD IN THE FAITH EVEN OUR END, [Phil. 1:6, I Pet. 4:19] so that we may believe the Gospel with all our heart, live holy Christian lives, trust God to lead us as He sees best, and be faithful unto death, that we may receive the crown of life.

QUESTIONS.—1. What do we pray for in this petition? 2. What do we mean by God's will in this petition? 3. How do we pray that God's will may be done? 4. Why is the will of God good and gracious? 5. How is God's will done without our prayer? 6. When do we do God's will? 7. What three things do we pray God to do? 8. What three wills oppose the will of God? 9. What do the devil, the world, and our own flesh seek? 10. Why do we pray God to strengthen us? 11. When do we remain steadfast in God's Word and in the faith?

SCRIPTURE VERSES.—I Tim. 2:4. Who will have all men to be saved, and to come unto the knowledge of the truth.

I Thess. 4:3. For this is the will of God, even your sanctification.

Rom. 8:17. And if children, then heirs; heirs of God, and joint heirs with Christ: if so be that we suffer with him, that we may be also glorified together.

Gal. 5:17. For the flesh lusteth against the Spirit, and the Spirit against the flesh: and these are contrary the one to the other; so that ye cannot do the things that ye would.

Eph. 6:11, 12. Put on the whole armour of God, that ye may be able to stand against the wiles of the devil. For we wrestle not against flesh and blood, but against principalities, against powers, against the rulers of the darkness of this world, against spiritual wickedness in high places.

READING.—Jesus in Gethsemane, Matt. 26:36-44.

CHAPTER XXVIII.
THE FOURTH PETITION.

Give us this day our daily bread.

What is meant by this Petition?

God gives, indeed, without our prayer, even to the wicked also, their daily bread; but we pray in this petition that He would make us sensible of His benefits, and enable us to receive our daily bread with thanksgiving.

What is implied in the words "our daily bread"?

All things that pertain to the wants and the support of this present life; such as food, raiment, money, goods, house and land, and other property; a believing spouse and good children; trustworthy servants and faithful magistrates; favorable seasons, peace and health; education and honor; true friends, good neighbors, and the like.

In this Petition we acknowledge that every good gift comes from God; [Jas. 1:17] and we pray that He would give us, day by day, those things which we need for our earthly support and comfort, and would make us content and thankful.

THE PETITION ITSELF.

While we are to pray first and chiefly for spiritual blessings, the Saviour here teaches us that we may and should pray for temporal benefits also.

GIVE. By praying God to *give* us our daily bread, we acknowledge that it comes from Him.[9] He is the absolute owner of all things, [I Cor. 10:26] and divides to all men as He will. All that we have is His gift. He gives it as a blessing upon our labor; hence, we must work as well as pray. [II Thess. 3:10] But without His blessing, our labor would be in vain. [Ps. 127:1] The farmer sows, but God gives the increase.

[Footnote 9: Compare this Petition with the First Article of the Creed and its Explanation.]

US. We are taught to pray not only for ourselves, but for others also. We should be concerned that they too may have their daily bread; and, when necessary, we should give them a portion of what God has first given to us, and thus become the means through which He supplies their wants. [Heb. 13:16]

THIS DAY. We are not to pray for "much goods for many years," but only for this one day's needful supply. When the morrow comes, if we are still alive, we are to pray again. [Matt.6:34+] We are to depend upon God from day to day. We are, indeed, to make a proper provision for our future, but we are not to give way to anxious, unbelieving care about it.

OUR. We ask for bread which we may call our own, bread honestly gotten, bread which God intends we shall have as a reward of our labor; not some one's else bread, and not such things as God, in His wisdom, sees fit to withhold from us.

DAILY BREAD. According to Luther's explanation in the Catechism, our daily bread includes

ALL THINGS WHICH PERTAIN TO THE WANTS AND THE SUPPORT OF THIS PRESENT

FOOD, RAIMENT, to supply our bodily wants;

MONEY, GOODS, HOUSE AND LAND, AND OTHER PROPERTY, by means of which we may procure the supply of our bodily wants;

A BELIEVING SPOUSE AND GOOD CHILDREN, that we may have a good Christian home;

TRUSTWORTHY SERVANTS AND FAITHFUL MAGISTRATES, that we may have the help and protection which we need for the enjoyment of our own;

FAVORABLE SEASONS, PEACE AND HEALTH, EDUCATION AND HONOR, TRUE FRIENDS,

While we pray in this petition that God would give us all the things enumerated above, *if He sees fit*, we should remember that He is still giving us our daily bread when He gives us only those things which we actually must have for the support of our life. [1 Tim. 6:8]

WHY WE PRAY THUS.

GOD GIVES INDEED, WITHOUT OUR PRAYER, EVEN TO THE WICKED [Matt. 5:45] ALSO THEIR DAILY BREAD; for God is good, and seeks to lead men to repentance by His goodness. [Rom. 2:4]

BUT WE PRAY IN THIS PETITION THAT HE WOULD MAKE US SENSIBLE OF HIS

AND ENABLE US TO RECEIVE OUR DAILY BREAD WITH THANKSGIVING. [Eph. 5:20+] Since all the blessings we enjoy are God's gifts, bestowed without any worthiness on our part, [Gen. 32:10] we pray that we may always receive them with thankful hearts, and express our gratitude with our lips and in our lives. We should give thanks at every meal, and in all our prayers.

Contentment. True thankfulness implies contentment with those gifts which God sees fit to bestow upon us. [Heb. 13:5+, 1 Tim. 6:6-8+] We must not murmur because He does not include in our daily bread some things which we desire to have; nor dare we permit the withholding of those things to prevent us from being truly thankful for the many benefits which God does bestow upon us.

QUESTIONS.—1. What do we acknowledge and for what do we pray in this petition? 2. Why do we pray God to "give"? 3. Why do we pray, "give *us*"? 4. Why do we pray "this day"? 5. Why do we say *our* daily bread? 6. What does daily bread include? 7. How much must God give us in order to answer this prayer for daily bread? 8. Why does God give, even to the wicked? 9. What should we bear in mind with respect to all our blessings? 10. How should we receive our daily bread? 11. How should we express our gratitude? 12. What is to be said about contentment?

SCRIPTURE VERSES.—Matt. 6:34. Take therefore no thought for the morrow: for the morrow shall take thought for the things of itself. Sufficient unto the day is the evil thereof.

Eph. 5:20. Giving thanks always for all things unto God and the Father in the name of our Lord Jesus Christ.

Heb. 13:5. Let your conversation be without covetousness: and be content with such things as ye have: for he hath said, I will never leave thee, nor forsake thee.

1 Tim. 6:6-8. But godliness with contentment is great gain. For we brought nothing into this world, and it is certain we can carry nothing out. And having food and raiment, let us be therewith content.

READING.—The Feeding of the Five Thousand, John 6:1-13.

CHAPTER XXIX.
THE FIFTH PETITION.
And forgive us our trespasses as we forgive those who trespass against us.

What is meant by this Petition?

We pray in this petition that our heavenly Father would not regard our sins, nor deny us our requests on account of them; for we are not worthy of anything for which we pray, and have not merited it; but that He would grant us all things through grace, although we daily commit much sin and deserve chastisement alone. We will, therefore, on our part both heartily forgive and also readily do good to those who may injure or offend us.

In this Petition we acknowledge our sinfulness, pray for forgiveness, and promise to forgive our fellow-men.

The word "And" connects this petition very closely with the preceding one. The daily forgiveness of our sins is as necessary for our souls as our daily bread is for our bodies.

AND FORGIVE US OUR TRESPASSES.

These words are at once a Confession of Sin, and a Prayer for Pardon.

1. A Confession. The praying of this petition presupposes a penitent state of heart. If we are not truly penitent, this petition is a mockery on our lips. We have need to confess our guilt, because

WE DAILY COMMIT MUCH SIN. [I John 4:8] If we are true Christians, we do not sin wilfully and intentionally. But with our best efforts, we still sin much through weakness, [Rom. 7:19] not only by commission, but still more by omission. Not a day passes by, in which we do not transgress God's law by thoughts and words and deeds. We often do the wrong and omit doing the right without even knowing that we have done so. [Ps. 19:12]

AND DESERVE CHASTISEMENT (Punishment) ALONE. Our sins make us guilty and deserving of punishment, even though they be sins of weakness. We must not excuse or extenuate them. God never excuses any one. But if we penitently confess our sins, He will forgive us for Jesus' sake. [Ps. 32:5+, I John 1:9]

2. A Prayer for Pardon. As in the fourth petition we daily pray "Give," so in this fifth petition we daily pray "Forgive." Since Jesus has taught us to pray thus, and we pray as God's children, this petition presupposes that we pray in faith. We pray as those who believe that God will be gracious and merciful to us for Jesus' sake.

WE PRAY IN THIS PETITION THAT OUR HEAVENLY FATHER WOULD NOT REGARD OUR

NOR DENY US OUR REQUESTS ON ACCOUNT OF THEM. If God should regard our sins, He would send only punishment upon us, [Ps. 130:3+, Ps.143:2] and not give us any of those benefits for which we ask in our prayer.

FOR WE ARE NOT WORTHY OF ANYTHING FOR WHICH WE PRAY, HAVE NOT MERITED

AS WE FORGIVE THOSE WHO TRESPASS AGAINST US.

3. A Promise to Forgive our Fellow-men. God's mercy to us must move as to be merciful to others. [Eph. 3:32] If it does not, God will withdraw His mercy from us, [Matt. 6:14, 15+] as the master withdrew his from the unmerciful servant in the parable. [Matt. 18:32-35] Forgiving others is not a merit which entitles us to receive God's forgiveness. It follows as a result of God's mercy to us. Because God so mercifully forgives us for Jesus' sake, we promise that

WE WILL, THEREFORE, ON OUR PART, BOTH HEARTILY FORGIVE AND ALSO READILY

QUESTIONS.—1. What three things do we do in this petition? 2. What is to be said about the close connection between this petition and the preceding one? 3. What does this petition presuppose? 4. Why do we need to confess our guilt to God? 5. Is sin ever excusable? 6. Why does this petition presuppose faith? 7. What do we pray God to do with our sins? 8. If God regarded our sins, how would He treat our requests? 9. Why do we promise to forgive others? 10. Why must we be willing to forgive them?

SCRIPTURE VERSES.—Ps. 32:5. I acknowledged my sin unto thee, and mine iniquity have I not hid. I said, I will confess my transgressions unto the LORD; and thou forgavest the iniquity of my sin.

Ps. 130:3. If thou, LORD, shouldest mark iniquities, O Lord, who shall stand?

Luke 15:18, 19. I will arise and go to my father, and will say unto him, Father, I have sinned against heaven, and before thee, and am no more worthy to be called thy son: make me as one of thy hired servants.

Matt. 6:14, 15. For if ye forgive men their trespasses, your heavenly Father will also forgive you: but if ye forgive not men their trespasses, neither will your Father forgive your trespasses.

READING.-The Unmerciful Servant, Matt. 18:23-35.

CHAPTER XXX.
THE SIXTH PETITION.

And lead us not into temptation.

What is meant by this Petition?

God, indeed, tempts no one to sin; but we pray in this petition that God would so guard and preserve us, that the devil, the world, and our own flesh may not deceive us, nor lead us into error and unbelief, despair, and other great and shameful sins; and that, though we may be thus tempted, we may nevertheless finally prevail and gain the victory.

As children of God we must not only seek forgiveness for past sins, but be anxious to avoid sin in the future. We therefore pray that, as far as is possible according to His gracious will, God would keep us from being tempted, and would give us strength to overcome when we are tempted.

If we are in earnest in praying this Petition, we will not run into temptation ourselves, [Matt. 4:7] nor lead others into it.

HOW WE ARE TEMPTED.

GOD INDEED TEMPTS NO ONE TO SIN: for He wishes us to do good, and not evil. But He leads us into circumstances in which we are *tried*, and must decide for or against Him, for good or for evil. This is the sense in which the Bible speaks of God as tempting persons. [Gen. 22:1] He tries or tests us. Remembering that we are weak, we pray in this petition that God would spare us such trials as much as is possible according to His will, and strengthen us in them, that we may be faithful.

The Devil, the World, and our own Flesh tempt us to Sin. These are the great enemies of our souls, who will lead us to destruction if we do not earnestly resist them and repel their temptations.

WHAT WE PRAY.

1. *That we may not be Deceived or Misled by these Enemies.*

WE PRAY IN THIS PETITION THAT GOD WOULD SO GUARD AND PRESERVE US, THAT

THE DEVIL, who puts evil thoughts into our hearts, [Gen. 3:4, 5, II Cor. 11:3]

THE WORLD (wicked persons in the world), [Prov. 1:10+, John 15:18] which tempts us by example, allurements, and threats,

AND OUR OWN FLESH (our natural heart), [Rom. 8:7+] which inclines and urges us to sin,

MAY NOT DECEIVE US, by promising us happiness in the paths of sin, while in reality such paths lead only to misery and destruction. [Matt. 7:13, 14+]

NOR LEAD US INTO ERROR AND UNBELIEF, and thus into ruin, since our salvation depends on believing the truth as it is in Jesus; nor into

DESPAIR; because we are lost if we despair of God's mercy, instead of believing His precious promises in Christ;

AND OTHER GREAT AND SHAMEFUL SINS, in addition to the error, unbelief, and despair mentioned above.

2. *That we may Overcome these Enemies and be saved,*
AND THAT, THOUGH WE MAY BE THUS TEMPTED, WE MAY NEVERTHELESS FINALLY

QUESTIONS.—1. Why do we pray this petition? 2. What do we mean by it? 3. If we are in earnest in praying it, what will we not do? 4. In what sense does God tempt? 5. Who tempts us to sin? 6. What do we pray against these enemies? 7. How does the devil tempt us? the world? our own flesh? 8. How do they try to deceive us? 9. Into what do they try to mislead us? 10. How long must we fight against these enemies? 11. If we fall, what should we do? 12. How may we overcome these foes? 13. When only shall we be completely victorious over them?

SCRIPTURE VERSES.—Prov. 1:10. My son, if sinners entice thee, consent thou not.

Rom. 8:7. Because the carnal mind is enmity against God: for it is not subject to the law of God, neither indeed can be.

Matt. 7:13, 14. Enter ye in at the strait gate: for wide is the gate, and broad is the way, that leadeth to destruction, and many there be which go in thereat: because strait is the gate, and narrow is the way, which leadeth unto life, and few there be that find it.

I Tim. 6:12. Fight the good fight of faith, lay hold on eternal life, whereunto thou art also called, and hast professed a good profession before many witnesses.

I Cor. 10:12. Let him that thinketh he standeth take heed lest he fall.

READING.—Peter denying the Lord, Luke 22:54-62; or, The Temptation of Jesus, Matt. 4:1-11.

CHAPTER XXXI.
THE SEVENTH PETITION.

But deliver us from evil.

What is meant by this Petition?

We pray in this petition, as in a summary, that our heavenly Father would deliver us from all manner of evil, whether it affect the body or the soul, property or character, and at last, when the hour of death shall arrive, grant us a happy end, and graciously take us from this world of sorrow to Himself in heaven.

As in the sixth Petition we pray to be preserved from sinning, so in this seventh Petition we pray to be delivered from all the evil which has come upon our race as a consequence of sin.[10] But this petition comes last, because we should be more anxious to be delivered from the sin itself, than from the evil results which follow upon it.

[Footnote 10: There is a very close connection between the last two petitions, marked by the word "But." "Temptation will not cease until deliverance from evil [and from the evil one] has come; and again, when deliverance from evil has come, temptation will cease to assail us."—Luekrs.]

WE PRAY IN PETITION AS IN A SUMMARY. All the petitions which precede it are included in this last one.

THAT OUR HEAVENLY FATHER WOULD DELIVER US FROM ALL MANNER OF EVIL:—

I. IN THIS WORLD.

WHETHER IT AFFECT THE BODY,—sickness, pain, hunger, thirst, destitution,
OR THE SOUL,—sin, impenitence, unbelief, sorrow, anxiety, care, despondency, insanity, and the like,
PROPERTY,—poverty, want, famine, fire, flood, wars, riots, etc.,
OR CHARACTER,—disgrace, slander, and the like.

How we pray for this Deliverance. God wills that we should sometimes suffer affliction, in order that our repentance and faith may be increased. [Isa. 48:10+, Rev. 3:19+, II Cor. 4:17, 18] Consequently, our prayer for deliverance from evil in this world is a prayer: 1. That, whenever it is possible according to His will, God would ward off affliction from us. 2. That He would give us grace to bear patiently those afflictions which He sends, [II Cor. 12:9+, Rom 8:28] and would make them a blessing in disguise for us. 3. That in His own time He would remove from us whatever distresses us. [I Sam. 2:6, 7]

We should not grow discouraged or despondent under affliction, but trust in God's mercy and bear our cross cheerfully. [Matt. 10:38] And we should see to it that we do not, by our own sin and folly, bring upon ourselves evils which might have been avoided.

II. IN THE NEXT WORLD.

In this world we shall have to endure some evils as long as we live. [John 16:33] But if we are faithful, God will not only overrule them all for our good, [Gen. 50:20] but will finally, at death, deliver us from all evil. [II Tim. 4:18]

AND AT LAST, WHEN THE HOUR OF DEATH SHALL ARRIVE, GRANT US A HAPPY END.
AND GRACIOUSLY TAKE US FROM THIS WORLD OF SORROW TO HIMSELF IN HEAVEN.

QUESTIONS.—1. What do we pray for in this petition? 2. What connection exists between the sixth and seventh petitions? 3. Why is this petition called a summary? 4. From what kind of evils do we suffer in this world? 5. How do we pray for deliverance from evil in this world? 6. When shall we be completely delivered from all evil? 7. What is to be said about a happy end? 8. Why shall we suffer from no evil in heaven?

SCRIPTURE VERSES.—Isa. 48:10. Behold, I have refined thee, but not with silver: I have chosen thee in the furnace of affliction.

Rev. 3:19. As many as I love, I rebuke and chasten: be zealous therefore, and repent.

II Cor. 12:9. And he said unto me, My grace is sufficient for thee: for my strength is made perfect in weakness.

Rom. 8:18. For I reckon that the sufferings of this present time are not worthy to be compared with the glory which shall be repealed in us.

Rev. 14:13. Blessed are the dead which die in the Lord from henceforth; Yea, saith the Spirit, that they may rest from their labours; and their works do follow them.

Rev. 21:4. These are they which came out of great tribulation, and have washed their robes, and made them, white in the blood of the Lamb. Therefore are they before the throne of God, and serve him day and night in his temple: and he that sitteth on the throne shall dwell among them.

READING.—The Rich Man and Lazarus, Luke 16:19-31.

CHAPTER XXXII.
THE CONCLUSION.

For Thine Is the kingdom, and the power, and the glory for ever and ever. Amen.
What is meant by the word "Amen"?

That I should be assured that such petitions are acceptable to our heavenly Father, and are heard by Him; for He Himself has commanded us to pray in this manner, and has promised that He will hear us. Amen, amen, that is, yea, yea, it shall be so.

In this Conclusion we give the reason why we address our prayer to our heavenly Father, and why we expect to be heard. It contains a Doxology, and an Amen.

THE DOXOLOGY.

FOR THINE IS THE KINGDOM: Thou art King and Lord of all; [I Tim. 1:17] from Thee all gifts must come. [Jas. 1:17]

AND THE POWER: with Thee nothing is impossible; [Luke 1:37] Thou art able to do abundantly above all that we ask or think. [Eph. 3:20]

AND THE GLORY: Thou art God alone, [Isa. 46:4] infinite in holiness, power, and love; to Thy name alone be all praise. [Ps. 115:1]

FOR EVER AND EVER. The kingdoms of earth and their glory pass away; but Thy kingdom and power and glory endure for evermore. [Dan. 4:3, Ps. 145:11-13+]

THE AMEN.

AMEN means Verily. By adding it to our prayer we express our assurance,

THAT SUCH PETITIONS ARE ACCEPTABLE TO OUR HEAVENLY FATHER AND ARE HEARD

FOR HE HIMSELF HAS TAUGHT US TO PRAY IN THIS MANNER, and to ask for these things,

AND HAS PROMISED THAT HE WILL HEAR US. [II Cor. 1:20] The promise is, that whatsoever we ask in Christ's name shall be given to us. [John 16:23] Hence we add at the end of our prayer: Amen, that is, it shall be so; God will answer our prayer. [Matt. 7:9-11]

QUESTIONS.—1. Why do we add the conclusion to the Lord's Prayer? 2. What two parts does the conclusion contain? 3. What do we mean by saying, "Thine is the kingdom"? the power? the glory? forever? 4. What does Amen mean? 5. Why do we add it to our prayer? 6. Why are we sure that these petitions are acceptable to our heavenly Father? 7. What promise have we with respect to our prayers?

SCRIPTURE VERSE.—Ps. 145:13. Thy kingdom is an everlasting kingdom, and thy dominion endureth throughout all generations.

READING.—Asking and Receiving, Luke 11:5-13.

CHAPTER XXXIII.
THE MEANS OF GRACE.

The spiritual blessings spoken of in the Creed and asked for in the Lord's Prayer are brought to us through the Means of Grace.

WHAT THEY ARE. The Means of Grace are: 1. The Word of God, 2. The Sacrament of Holy Baptism, 3. The Sacrament of the Altar. They are called the means of grace, because they are the means or vehicles through which God's grace comes to us. It is through the Word of God and the Sacraments that the Holy Spirit does His work in us.

THE WORD OF GOD.

THE CHIEF MEANS OF GRACE is the Word of God. [I Pet. 1:23] For through it the Holy Spirit "calls, enlightens, sanctifies, and preserves us in the true faith." Even in the Sacraments, the principal thing is the Word of God with its command and promise; and without the Word of God there would be no sacrament.

ITS POWER. The Holy Spirit is always in the Word, and gives it saving power. Through the Law and the Gospel which the Word contains, He brings to repentance and faith all those persons who do not wilfully resist His grace. [Heb. 4:12] Through it He not only tells us what to do, but gives us the power to obey. [Eph 2:4, 5] Because He is in the

Word, "it is the power of God unto salvation to every one that believeth." [Rom 1:16] (Compare what is said concerning the Bible in Chapter I., and concerning the Work of the Holy Spirit in Chapter XX.)

THE SACRAMENTS.

WHAT A SACRAMENT IS. A sacrament is a holy ordinance, instituted by Christ, in which invisible heavenly gifts are bestowed upon us through the use of visible earthly elements.

HOW MANY THERE ARE. In the sense in which we use the word "Sacrament" there are only two holy ordinances to which the name may be applied; namely, Baptism and the Lord's Supper. For these are the only two which possess the three essentials of a sacrament: 1. The Command of Christ; 2. The Use of Earthly Elements; 3. The Communication of a Heavenly Gift.[11]

[Footnote 11: The Roman Catholic Church teaches that there are seven sacraments: Baptism, Confirmation, Confession, the Lord's Supper, Ordination, Marriage, and Extreme Unction. But five of these lack one or more of the essentials of a sacrament enumerated above.]

OLD TESTAMENT TYPES. The rite of Circumcision, practised in Old Testament times, was a type of Baptism; and the Passover was a type of the Lord's Supper.

THEIR PURPOSE. The sacraments have been given to us in order that they might bring a special comfort to our souls, in addition to the comfort which we find in God's Word. For the Grace of God which is offered to all men in the Word, is brought and sealed to each believer *individually* in the sacraments. My baptism assures me that all the blessings of Christ's redemption are meant for *me*: and the Lord's Supper assures me that Christ's body and blood were given and shed for *me* for the remission of *my* sins.

FAITH NECESSARY. Without faith, no one can obtain any benefit from the sacraments. But he who believes receives the heavenly gifts offered in them, and has the blessed assurance that he is a child of God and an heir of heaven.

QUESTIONS.—1. How are the spiritual blessings spoken of in the Creed and asked for in the Lord's Prayer brought to us? 2. What are the Means of Grace? 3. Why are they so called? 4. What is the chief means of grace? 5. Why does the Word of God possess saving power? 6. What is a Sacrament? 7. How many Sacraments are there? 8. What are the three essentials of a sacrament? 9. What is the purpose of the sacraments? 10. Does every one who receives the sacraments derive a benefit from them?

SCULPTURE READING.—The Man Born Blind, John 9:1-7.

PART IV.

CHAPTER XXXIV.
THE SACRAMENT OF HOLY BAPTISM

I. *What is Baptism?*

Baptism is not simply water, but it is the water comprehended in God's command, and connected with God's Word.

What is that Word of God?

It is that which our Lord Jesus Christ spoke, as it is recorded in the last chapter of Matthew, verse 19: "Go ye, and teach (make disciples of) all nations, baptizing them in the name of the Father and of the Son and of the Holy Ghost."

WHAT BAPTISM IS.

Baptism consists in applying water to a person "in the name of the Father and of the Son and of the Holy Ghost," as Christ has commanded. [Matt. 28:19]

BAPTISM IS NOT SIMPLY WATER. In one sense, indeed, the water used in baptism is simply ordinary water from well, cistern, or stream; [Acts 8:36] but when used in baptism it ceases to be simply water, and possesses special value and power, because

IT IS THE WATER COMPREHENDED IN GOD'S COMMAND. The water of baptism is a water which God has commanded us to use,—His command being, "Go ye and make disciples of all nations, baptizing them," etc.

AND CONNECTED WITH GOD'S WORD. In baptism, water is applied "in the name of the Father and of the Son and of the Holy Ghost"; and thus it is used in connection, with the very words of Christ Himself. The water and the Word together make the sacrament.

ITS NECESSITY. Baptism is necessary for all, because Christ has commanded that all should be baptized, and has connected the blessing of salvation with this sacrament. [Matt. 16:16] Those who despise it and refuse to be baptized, cannot be saved. But if any person should desire baptism and be unable to obtain it, he would not on that account be lost. It is not the lack of baptism, but the despising of baptism that condemns.

Baptism is to be administered by the pastor. But if there should be extreme peril of death before a minister could possibly arrive, any member of the Church may baptize. Such lay-baptism, however, should afterwards be announced in church, and be declared valid.

WHO ARE TO BE BAPTIZED.

The command of Christ to "make disciples" includes "all nations." All those persons, therefore, who are willing to become disciples are to be baptized; namely, adults who have received the proper religious instruction and profess faith in Christ, and children whom competent sponsors present for baptism.

INFANT BAPTISM. Infants should be baptized at a very early age, and thus be received into God's covenant as His children. Since they cannot be instructed before baptism, they should be carefully instructed afterwards [Matt. 28:20] and be brought up in the nurture and admonition of the Lord, [Eph. 6:4] so that they may always remain faithful and obedient children of God.

SPONSORS answer the questions for the child at its baptism, and promise to see to it that the child is properly instructed and trained in the Christian religion. Sponsors must themselves be members in good standing in the Church.

WHY CHILDREN SHOULD BE BAPTIZED.[12] As children were received into the Old Testament covenant by the rite of circumcision, which was a type of baptism, so God desires that they shall be received into the New Testament covenant by baptism. Some of the reasons for infant baptism are the following:—

[Footnote 12: Baptists sometimes argue against infant baptism on the basis of the Scripture passage: "Go ye and teach all nations, baptizing them," etc., claiming that Christ says first teach and then baptize. But, as a matter of fact, Christ mentions baptizing before teaching in this passage. For in its correct translation, as given in the Revised Version of the English Bible, it reads, "Go ye therefore, and *make disciples* of all the nations, *baptizing* them into the name of the Father and of the Son and of the Holy Ghost; *teaching* them to observe all things whatsoever I commanded you." If the order in which the two words "baptize" and "teach" occur in this passage proved anything with respect to the baptism of infants, it would prove that they *should* be baptized. For in the case of children, baptizing comes first and teaching follows, just as in the passage quoted.]

1. Children form part of the "nations" whom Christ commanded His disciples to baptize.

2. They are by nature sinful and need God's grace as well as adults. [John 3:5, 6, Job 14:4] While they have not yet committed any conscious transgressions, they have

inherited a sinful heart, and the germs of sin in them will soon grow into actual transgressions.

3. Christ has commanded that little children should be brought to Him, and we obey this command by baptizing them and teaching them. [Luke 18:16]

4. Christ says of children, "Of such is the kingdom of God": [Mark 10:14, 15+] and they have a right, therefore, to receive that sacrament by which we enter God's kingdom.

5. The promise of God's grace is given to children as well as to adults. [Acts 2:39]

6. Children have capacity for faith. [Matt. 18:6]

7. The apostles baptized whole families. [Acts 16:33]

HOW BAPTISM IS TO BE ADMINISTERED.

In His command to baptize, Christ does not specify any mode of baptism. It may be performed in any one of three ways; namely, by sprinkling, pouring, or immersion. One mode of baptism is just as valid as the others. The most convenient mode, the one best adapted to all circumstances, and the one most widely used in the Christian Church, is by pouring or sprinkling. Immersion is not advisable in our climate, and in many cases, such as severe sickness, it could not possibly be employed.

IMMERSION NOT ESSENTIAL. The word "baptize" does not necessarily mean to immerse, as the Baptists claim. When the Saviour instituted this sacrament, He did not coin a new word, but employed one already in use. The original Greek word from which our English word "baptize" is derived, is used in the New Testament in the sense of washing [Mark 7:4] and sprinkling. [I Cor. 10:2] The baptism of the three thousand on the day of Pentecost [Acts 2:41] and of the Philippian jailor [Acts 16:33] could hardly have been by immersion, on account of the scarcity of water available for such a purpose. When Jesus was baptized, He "came up out of the water"; [Matt. 3:16] but it is quite probable that He stood in the stream while John poured water on His head.

THE ESSENCE OF BAPTISM consists in applying water "in the name of the Father and of the Son and of the Holy Ghost"; and its gracious effect depends, not on the amount of water that is used, but on the Word of God with which the water is connected.

QUESTIONS.—1. What does baptism consist in? 2. Why is baptism not simply water? 3. What is meant by "water comprehended in God's command"? 4. What is meant by "water connected with God's Word"? 5. What is to be said about the necessity of baptism? 6. Who are to be baptized? 7. What is to be said about infant baptism? 8. Who may be sponsors, and what is their duty? 9. Give some reasons for infant baptism. 10. What is to be said about the mode of baptism? 11. Why is immersion not essential? 12. In what does the essence of baptism consist?

SCRIPTURE VERSES.—John 3:5, 6. Jesus answered, Verily, verily, I say unto thee, Except a man be born of water and of the Spirit, he cannot enter into the kingdom of God. That which is born of the flesh is flesh; and that which is born of the Spirit is spirit.

Mark 10:14, 15. But when Jesus saw it, he was much displeased, and said unto them, Suffer the little children to come unto me, and forbid them not: for of such is the kingdom of God. Verily I say unto you, Whosoever shall not receive the kingdom of God as a little child, he shall not enter therein.

READING.-The Baptism of Jesus, Matt. 3:13-17.

CHAPTER XXXV.

II. *What gifts or benefits does Baptism confer?*

It works forgiveness of sins, delivers from death and the devil, and confers everlasting salvation on all who believe, as the Word and promise of God declare.

What are such words and promises of God?

Those which our Lord Jesus Christ spoke, as they are recorded in the last chapter of Mark, verse 16: "He that believeth and is baptized shall be saved; but he that believeth not shall be damned."

THE BENEFITS OF BAPTISM.

Baptism is God's means of receiving us into His covenant, and opening up to us all the treasures of Christ's redemption. Through this sacrament He adopts us as His children and receives us into membership in His Church. [Gal. 3:36, 27+] We are baptized in (into) the name of the Father (who sent His Son to save us), and of the Son (who died to redeem us), and of the Holy Ghost (who applies Christ's redemption to our souls). Therefore every baptized person may say, "God is *my* Father, Christ is *my* Redeemer, the Holy Ghost is *my* Sanctifier, and all the benefits of Christ's redemption are offered to *me*." Hence we declare of baptism, that

IT WORKS FORGIVENESS OF SINS, [Acts 2:38+, Acts 22:16, Eph. 5:25, 26] DELIVERS FROM DEATH AND THE DEVIL, AND CONFERS EVERLASTING SALVATION. These are the very benefits which Christ has acquired for me by His innocent sufferings and death (see Article II, of the Creed, Chapter XIX.). And since I have been "baptized into Christ's death," [Rom 6:3+] all these benefits belong to me if I only accept them by faith. [Mark 16:16] I am regarded by God as having already suffered the full penalty of my sins in Christ's death, and for His sake I am pardoned and saved.

ON ALL WHO BELIEVE. Faith is the hand with which we grasp and hold fast the treasures of God's grace offered in this sacrament. The benefits are offered to every one who is baptized, but they are accepted and possessed only by him who believes.

AS THE WORD AND PROMISE OF GOD DECLARE. The benefits belong to all who are baptized and believe, because God has said so. [Numb. 23:19] He has promised, "He that believeth and is baptized shall be saved."

WITHOUT FAITH baptism will not save any one. "He that believeth not shall be damned" even though he is baptized. For while such a person has been adopted as God's child, he is a disobedient and rebellious child, and therefore is disinherited, and loses the heavenly inheritance [Pet. 1:4] which would have been his, if he had remained faithful.

BAPTISM PERMANENT. Baptism, once properly administered, is not to be repeated. It is a permanent covenant between God and us. While men are often unfaithful to their covenant, God never is. [II Cor. 1:20, Rom. 3:3] He bestows the blessings of baptism on all who comply with its conditions. Having received us by baptism as His children, He ever afterwards remains our loving heavenly Father, to whom we may turn with fullest confidence. And if any who have fallen from grace repent and seek His mercy, they find Him standing with open arms to receive them. [Luke 15:11-24] Such persons need not be re-baptized; their old baptism stands. A rebellious son who repents needs not to be re-adopted, but needs only to be forgiven.

III. *How can water produce such great effects?*

It is not the water, indeed, that produces these effects, but the Word of God which accompanies and is connected with the water, and our faith which relies on the Word of God connected with the water. For the water without the Word of God is simply water, and no baptism. But when connected with the Word of God, it is a baptism, that is, a gracious water of life and a washing of regeneration in the Holy Ghost; as St. Paul says to Titus in the third chapter, verses 5-8: "According to His mercy He saved us, by the washing of regeneration, and renewing of the Holy Ghost; which He shed on us abundantly through Jesus Christ, our Saviour; that being justified by His grace, we should be made heirs according to the hope of eternal life. This is a faithful saying."

WHY BAPTISM HAS POWER TO CONFER SUCH BENEFITS.

IT IS NOT THE WATER, INDEED, THAT PRODUCES THESE EFFECTS. Water alone cannot wash away sins. Yet the water of baptism is necessary, because Christ has commanded its use, and has connected the promise of salvation with it.

BUT THE WORD OF GOD WHICH ACCOMPANIES AND IS CONNECTED WITH THE WATER.[13]

[Footnote 13: The story of Naaman the leper (II Kings 5:8-14) illustrates how water, the Word of God, and faith can produce great effects. It was not the water of the Jordan that cured Naaman; yet he could not have been cured without the water, because the promise of healing was connected with its use. When he *believed* the Word of promise and used the water as he was commanded, he was healed. So the water, the Word, and our faith, which trusts in the Word, cleanse us from the leprosy of sin.]

IT IS A GRACIOUS WATER OF LIFE, because the Word and promise of God, which are connected with it, give it power to bestow life and salvation on all who believe.

AND A "WASHING OF REGENERATION" in the Holy Ghost, because it is the means through which the Holy Ghost causes us to be "born again," as God's children.

QUESTIONS.—1. What does God do for us through baptism? 2. What may every baptized person say? 3. What benefits does baptism confer? 4. Who has acquired these benefits for you, and how? 5. Why do they become yours through baptism? 6. What has faith to do with the reception of these benefits? 7. How do we know that baptism confers all these benefits on all who believe? 8. What is to be said about those who are baptized but do not believe? 9. What is to be said about the permanence of baptism? 10. Why has baptism power to confer such great benefits? 11. Why is it a "gracious water of life," and a "washing of regeneration"?

SCRIPTURE VERSES.—Gal. 3:26, 27. For ye are all the children of God by faith in Christ Jesus. For as many of you as have been baptized into Christ, have put on Christ.

Acts 2:38. Then Peter said unto them, Repent, and be baptized every one of you in the name of Jesus Christ for the remission of sins, and ye shall receive the gift of the Holy Ghost.

Rom. 6:3. Know ye not, that so many of us as were baptized into Jesus Christ were baptized into his death?

Numb. 23:19. God is not a man, that he should lie; neither the son of man, that he should repent: hath he said, and shall he not do it? or hath he spoken, and shall he not make it good?

READING.—Naaman, II Kings 5:1-14.

CHAPTER XXXVI.

IV. *What does such baptising with water signify?*

It signifies that the old Adam in us is to be drowned and destroyed by daily sorrow and repentance, together with all sins and evil lusts; and that again the new man should daily come forth and rise, that shall live in the presence of God in righteousness and purity forever.

Where is it so written?

St. Paul, in the epistle to the Romans, chapter 6, verse 4, says: "We are buried with Christ by baptism into death; that like as He was raised up from the dead by the glory of the Father, even so we also should walk in newness of life."

THE DUTY WHICH BAPTISM IMPOSES.

Baptism bestows upon us the great privilege of being children of God; but it also imposes upon us the duty to live and act as God's children. Every one who is baptized promises, either with his own lips or through his sponsors, that he will live thus. God is always faithful to His part of the baptismal covenant; we should always be faithful to ours. Our duty is two-fold:—

1. THE OLD ADAM IN US IS TO BE DROWNED, DESTROYED BY DAILY SORROW AND

2. THE NEW MAN SHOULD DAILY COME FORTH AND RISE, THAT SHALL LIVE IN THE CONFIRMATION.

The rite of confirmation is closely connected with the baptism of children. For the children who have been baptized are afterwards to be taught "to observe all things whatsoever Christ has commanded"; [Matt. 28:20] and, when they have reached an age at which they are able to examine themselves, they should be confirmed.

PRECEDED BY INSTRUCTION. Confirmation is to be preceded by thorough instruction in the doctrines and duties of the Christian religion. In addition to the instruction received in the home and the Sunday-school, those who desire to be confirmed are specially instructed in the catechetical class by the pastor. Confirmation is the Church's testimony that the catechumens have received the necessary instruction to fit them for intelligent and earnest participation in the full privileges of Church membership. This instruction is the principal thing, and without it confirmation would lose its meaning.

WHAT CONFIRMATION IS. In confirmation the catechumen makes no new promises, but repeats with his own lips the confession of faith and the promise of faithfulness to Christ which were made for him by his sponsor at his baptism. Thereupon the minister lays his hand upon the head of each catechumen, and the minister and congregation pray that God would give to each His Holy Spirit to keep him in the faith and to cause him to grow in holiness.

WHY WE CONFIRM. Confirmation is not commanded in the Scriptures, but is a useful ordinance of the Church. It does not make us members of the Church; for we become members by baptism; but it admits us to *communicant* membership in the Church. Those who have been confirmed are admitted to the Lord's Supper. They are also entitled to act as sponsors at the baptism of children. The right to vote depends upon the constitution of the particular congregation.

QUESTIONS.—1. What duty does baptism impose? 2. In what two-fold way is this duty to be performed? 3. What is meant by "the old Adam in us"? 4. What shall be done with our old sinful self? 5. How shall we succeed in gaining the mastery over it? 6. What is meant by the "new man"? 7. What does our new self prompt us to do? 8. What should the new man in us do? 9. What is to be done with children who have been baptized? 10. By what is confirmation to be preceded? 11. What is to be said about the importance of this instruction? 12. Tell what confirmation is? 13. Why do we confirm? 14. What privileges does confirmation confer?

SCRIPTURE VERSES.—Eph. 4:22. That ye put off concerning the former conversation the old man, which is corrupt according to the deceitful lusts.

Gal. 5:24. And they that are Christ's have crucified the flesh with the affections and lusts.

Eph. 4:24. And that ye put on the new man, which after God is created in righteousness and true holiness.

Phil. 3:12. Not as though I had already attained, either were already perfect: but I follow after, if that I may apprehend that for which also I am apprehended of Christ Jesus.

READING.—The Lame Man of Bethesda, John 5:1-14.

CHAPTER XXXVII.
THE SACRAMENT OF THE ALTAR.

I. *What is the Sacrament of the Altar?*

It is the true body and blood of our Lord Jesus Christ, under the bread and wine, given unto us Christians to eat and to drink, as it was instituted by Christ Himself.

Where is it so written?
The holy evangelists, Matthew, Mark, and Luke, together with St. Paul, write thus: "Our Lord Jesus Christ, the same night in which He was betrayed, took bread: and when He had given thanks, He broke it, and gave it to His disciples and said, Take, eat; this is My body, which is given for you: this do in remembrance of Me. After the same manner also He took the cup when He had supped, gave thanks, and gave it to them, saying, Drink ye all of it: this cup is the New Testament in My blood, which is shed for you, for the remission of sins: this do, as oft as ye drink it, in remembrance of Me."

ITS NAMES. This sacrament is called: 1. The Sacrament of the Altar, because it is administered at the altar. 2. The Lord's Supper, because it was instituted by the *Lord* while the disciples were eating the Passover *Supper*. 3. The Table of the Lord, because the Lord here gives food and drink to our souls. 4. The Communion, because it is a communion of bread and wine with the body and blood of Christ, a communion of believers with Christ, and a communion of believers with one another. 5. The Eucharist—a name derived from a Greek word meaning to give thanks—because the administration of the Lord's Supper is attended with thanksgiving.

WHAT THE SACRAMENT OF THE ALTAR IS.
The Lord's Supper was instituted by OUR LORD JESUS CHRIST THE SAME NIGHT IN WHICH HE WAS BETRAYED, while He and the disciples were eating the Passover Supper. [I Cor. 11:23-25, Matt. 26:26-28, Mark 14:22-24, Luke 22:19-20] What the Lord's Supper is, we learn from the words of Christ Himself as given by the evangelists, Matthew, Mark, and Luke, and by St. Paul.

THE EARTHLY ELEMENTS. The Lord TOOK BREAD, AND WHEN HE HAD GIVEN THANKS, HE BROKE IT AND GAVE IT TO HIS DISCIPLES. AFTER THE SAME MANNER ALSO HE TOOK THE CUP containing the wine, WHEN HE HAD SUPPED, GAVE THANKS, AND GAVE IT TO THEM. The earthly elements used in this sacrament are, therefore, bread and wine. The wafers which are generally used in Lutheran Churches are unleavened bread—the kind which Christ used—because at the time of the Passover no other but unleavened bread dared be used by the Jews. The wine which Christ used was real wine, not unfermented grape juice. We are not permitted to substitute anything else in place of the earthly elements used by Christ in instituting this sacrament.

THE BODY AND BLOOD OF CHRIST. When Christ gave His disciples the bread, HE SAID, TAKE, EAT; THIS IS MY BODY, WHICH IS GIVEN FOR YOU. When He gave them the wine, HE SAID, DRINK YE ALL OF IT; THIS CUP IS THE NEW TESTAMENT IN MY BLOOD, WHICH IS SHED FOR YOU FOR THE REMISSION OF SINS. Consequently, when we receive the bread in this sacrament, we receive also the body of Christ; and when we receive the wine, we receive also the blood of Christ. And we say of the Sacrament of the Altar, that

IT IS THE TRUE BODY AND BLOOD OF OUR LORD CHRIST, UNDER (along with) THE BREAD AND WINE, GIVES UNTO US CHRISTIANS TO EAT TO AS IT WAS INSTITUTED BY HIMSELF. The bread and wine *do not simply represent* the body and blood of Christ (Zwingli's view). The bread and wine are *not changed into* the body and blood of Christ (the Roman Catholic view, or transubstantiation). The bread and wine are not united with the body and blood of Christ into a third substance different from both (consubstantiation). The bread and wine remain real bread and wine throughout the administration of the Lord's Supper. [I Cor. 11:28] But there is a communion of the bread and wine with the body and blood of Christ, [I Cor. 10:16+] so that when the communicant receives the bread he receives also the body of Christ, and when he receives the wine, he receives also the blood of Christ. The bread and wine are the earthly vehicles through which the heavenly gift of Christ's body and blood, which were given, and shed for us for the remission of sins, are communicated to us. [I Cor. 10:28, 29]

DOCTRINES COMPARED. The Reformed, Lutheran, and Roman Catholic doctrines of the Lord's Supper may be compared and illustrated thus:—

Reformed. Lutheran. Roman Catholic.

Bread. Bread-Body. Body. Wine. Wine-Blood. Blood.

According to the Reformed view, only bread and wine are present; according to the Roman Catholic[14] view, only the body and blood of Christ are present; according to the Lutheran and Scriptural doctrine, both the bread and wine and the body and blood of Christ are present in the Holy Supper, and are received by every communicant.

[Footnote 14: Because of its false doctrine concerning the Lord's Supper, the Roman Catholic Church has fallen into these additional errors: 1. The Sacrifice of the Mass, in which the priest, by blessing the bread and wine, is supposed to turn them into the body and blood of Christ, and thus to offer an unbloody sacrifice of Christ which is as effective as Christ's death on the cross. 2. The Withholding of the cup from the laity, lest a single drop of Christ's blood should be spilled. 3. The Elevation of the Host, in which the wafer or host is adored as the body of Christ.]

A GREAT MYSTERY. The Lord's Supper is a great mystery; but also a great comfort. We cannot understand how Christ can give us His body and blood in this sacrament. But it is the part of faith to take the Saviour at His word. This the Lutheran Church does in her doctrine.

QUESTIONS.—1. By what different names is this sacrament known and why? 2. From what do we learn what the Lord's Supper is? 3. What is to be said about the earthly elements? 4. When Christ gave His disciples the bread and the wine, what did He say? 5. What do we receive, therefore, in the Lord's Supper? 6. What is to be said about Zwingli's view? 7. What is to be said about the Roman Catholic view, and what is it called? 8. What other false doctrine besides these two is to be rejected? 9. How may the Reformed, Lutheran, and Roman Catholic doctrines of the Lord's Supper be compared? 10. Is the true doctrine to be rejected because we do not understand it?

SCRIPTURE VERSES.—I Cor. 10:16. The cup of blessing which we bless, is it not the communion of the blood of Christ? The bread which we break, is it not the communion of the body of Christ?

READING.—The Institution of the Lord's Supper, Matt. 26:17-30.

II. *What benefits are derived from such eating and drinking?*

They are pointed out in these words: "given and shed for you, for the remission of sins"; namely, through these words, the remission of sins, life and salvation are granted unto us in the sacrament. For where there is remission of sins, there are also life and salvation.

THE BENEFITS DERIVED FROM THE LORD'S SUPPER.

The benefits offered in this sacrament and bestowed upon all who receive it In faith ARE POINTED OUT IN THESE WORDS of the institution: "GIVEN AND SHED FOR YOU, FOR THE REMISSION OF SINS." Accordingly, the benefits are: "REMISSION OF SINS, LIFE AND SALVATION." For while only the remission (forgiveness) of sins is mentioned in the institution, yet WHERE THERE IS REMISSION OF SINS, THERE ARE ALSO LIFE AND SALVATION. [Rom. 6:22] The Lord's Supper confers all the benefits which Christ secured by His sufferings and death. [Eph. 1:7] Each communicant is assured by the words of Christ Himself that the body which he receives along with the bread was given for *him*, and that the blood which he receives along with the wine was shed for *him*, for the remission of *his* sins. The promise of grace and forgiveness held out to all in the Gospel is thus brought home to each individual in the Lord's Supper. Each believing communicant is individually assured that Christ is *his* Saviour, and that *he* has the forgiveness of sins, life, and salvation through Christ's death.

III. *How can the bodily eating and drinking produce such great effects?*

The eating and the drinking, indeed, do not produce them; but the words which stand here, namely, "given and shed for you for the remission of sins." These words are, besides the bodily eating and drinking, the chief things in the sacrament; and he who believes these words has that which they declare and set forth; namely, the remission of sins.

WHY THE LORD'S SUPPER HAS POWER TO CONFER SUCH BENEFITS. THE EATING AND THE DRINKING, INDEED, DO NOT PRODUCE SUCH GREAT EFFECTS.
BUT THE WORDS WHICH STAND HERE, "GIVEN AND SHED FOR YOU, FOR THE
AND HE WHO BELIEVES THESE WORDS HAS THAT WHICH THEY DECLARE, [Matt. 8:13] NAMELY, THE REMISSION OF SINS. Forgiveness of sins, life, and salvation are offered to all who partake of this sacrament, but they are accepted and possessed only by those who believe. The impenitent and unbelieving, if they come to the Lord's Table, receive the body and blood of Christ also, but they receive it to their condemnation, because they do not receive it with a penitent and believing heart. [I Cor 11:29+]

IV. *Who is it that receives this sacrament worthily?*
Fasting and bodily preparation are, indeed, a good external discipline; but he is truly worthy and well prepared who believes these words: "given and shed for you, for the remission of sins." But he who does not believe these words or who doubts, is unworthy and unfit; for the words "for you" require truly believing hearts.

HOW THE LORD'S SUPPER IS TO BE RECEIVED.
Those who come to the Lord's Table must prepare themselves to come *worthily*, if they would receive the benefits offered in this sacrament. [I Cor. 11:28+, II Cor. 13:5]
FASTING AND BODILY PREPARATION ARE INDEED A GOOD EXTERNAL DISCIPLINE.
HE IS TRULY WORTHY AND WELL-PREPARED, WHO BELIEVES THESE WORDS, "GIVEN,

THE CONFESSIONAL SERVICE. The administration of the Lord's Supper is always preceded by the service of confession and absolution, so that those who desire to come to the Lord's Table may prepare themselves to come worthily. At this service we make a public confession of our sins, of our faith in Christ our Saviour, and of our earnest determination by God's grace to lead a holy life. Since Christ has conferred upon the Church the Power of the Keys, saying, "Whosoever sins ye remit, they are remitted, unto them, and whosoever sins ye retain, they are retained," [John 20:23] the minister uses this power and pronounces the absolution. In the name of the Father and of the Son and of the Holy Ghost he declares to all who truly repent and believe, the entire forgiveness of all their sins. On the other hand, to all who are impenitent and unbelieving he declares, that their sins are retained so long as they do not come to true repentance and faith.

Our Church does not require private confession of sins to the pastor; but if any one is troubled in conscience, and desires to make confession to the minister and to obtain the comfort of an absolution pronounced specially upon him, there is provision for private confession and absolution. Such private confessions are regarded by every true pastor as sacredly confidential. (See the "Questions on Confession," which form one of the additions to the Five Principal Parts of the Catechism.)

QUESTIONS.—1. What are the benefits derived from the Lord's Supper? 2. Where are they pointed out? 3. How have these benefits been secured for us? 4. What assurance does each communicant receive? 5. Why has the Lord's Supper power to confer such benefits? 6. Does every communicant receive the benefits offered? 7. How is the Lord's Supper to be received? 8. What is to be said about fasting as a preparation? 9.

What is the true preparation? 10. What is meant by receiving the Lord's Supper worthily? 11. Describe the confessional service? 12. What is to be said about private confession and absolution?

SCRIPTURE VERSES.—I Cor. 11:29. For he that eateth and drinketh unworthily, eateth and drinketh damnation to himself, not discerning the Lord's body.

I Cor. 11:28. But let a man examine himself, and so let him eat of that bread, and drink of that cup.

Joel 2:13. And rend your heart, and not your garments, and turn unto the LORD your God: for he is gracious and merciful, slow to anger, and of great kindness, and repenteth him of the evil.

Ps. 51:17. A broken and a contrite heart, O God, thou wilt not despise.

Matt. 11:28. Come unto me, all ye that labour and are heavy laden, and I will give you rest.

READING.—The Wedding Garment, Matt. 22:1-14.

Printed in the USA
CPSIA information can be obtained
at www.ICGtesting.com
LVHW051800081224
798648LV00019B/95